The LOCKS HEATH *Story*

——►•○•◄——

"This book is dedicated to the memory of Charlotte Hornby, whose bequest enabled St.John's Church, Locks Heath to be built and endowed."

——►•○•◄——

First published September 1995.

Published by Peter Jeffs, Titchfield, Hants.
Designed and produced by Phil Broadway.
Printed and bound in Great Britain by Bishops Printers, Southsea, Hants.

ISBN 0 9526760 0 1

PREHISTORIC

[T]o view the pre-history of an area as small as the region now known as [Loc]ks Heath it is necessary to view it in the wider context of South-West [Ha]mpshire as a whole.

[We] know that men are first thought to have reached southern Britain at [a ti]me of dramatic climatic changes. There is positive evidence that [mo]dern man's predecessors 'Homo erectus' arrived in bands crossing [a] land bridge from the continents following the herds of game upon [wh]ich they were largely dependent, about 200,000 B.C.

[Too]ls as evidence of the crude flint technology and the human acitivity [of t]hat time have been found at Hill Head and Titchfield. Vast quantities [of t]he hand axes in use up to 70,000 B.C. have been found, many [com]ing from the gravel workings near Hook and Warsash.

[Flin]t sickles and jadeite axes used by the first farmers have been found [and] an Iron Age site uncovered at Brownwich Farm produced evidence [of t]he metal-working carried out in support of the maritime trade at the [near]by shore in the first century A.D.

[The] Roman invaders laid the first major road along the 27 miles from [Winc]hester to Bitterne. During the next three centuries of Roman rule [the] road served a number of small settlements, farms and villas in the [wid]e coastal strip. A network of minor unmetalled tracks were [esta]blished in our region for cross-country communication.

[The] isolated peasant households in our region had a heavy burden in [tax i]n both kind and cash, and the farmers were obliged to adjust their [lives] to the production of a huge surplus.

[Angl]o-saxons and Jutes were the next identifiable settlers in the fifth and sixth centuries. For several hundred years the Hampshire Jutes remained distinct from their Saxon neighbours on either side in Wessex and Sussex.

The Jutes, with the South Saxons, were the last of the English to be converted to Christianity. The story of church building begins with Saint Wilfred who having been exiled from the Diocese of York, landed in Sussex in 681 A.D. and found the people still pagan.

Heathen gods were generally worshipped until the seventh century when the influence of St. Wilfred and Bishop Birinus was felt. Bede reported that Wessex was converted to Christianity by Bishop Birinus who arrived in 634 A.D. having been commissioned by Pope Honorius to preach the Gospel 'in the distant lands beyond the English dominions where no other teacher had been before him'.

Parish churches were not built immediately and open-air preaching was carried out in our area by priests from the new religious community established at Titchfield. St. Peter's Titchfield is clearly identified as being of early Saxon origin from the late seventh century, built as a "minster church" in 680 A.D. in an area which was shown in Domesday in 1086 as being a large royal estate.

The Saxon parish of Titchfield was large and covered the area bounded by the River Hamble in the west to the River Meon in the east, and northwards from the Solent to Wickham.

This ancient parish continued until 1232 when Peter de Roche Bishop of Winchester decided to establish an abbey near the village. To found the abbey he invited a group of canons from the abbey of Halesowen in Gloucestershire and the Manor was endowed with a number of local estates by the King.

The income and the land provided all that was necessary for the simple life in the abbey. A single-minded dedication to a life of prayer, poverty and work ensured that the abbey prospered. The abbott and the canons accumulated over 10,000 acres including a number of manors during the 300 years of their occupancy.

The General Famine of 1315-17 and Black Death of 1348 severely reduced the population farming the estates and their arable land. The national estimates of the time showed that up to 80% of the urban community stretching to the coast had perished.

By the thirteenth century the community had grown again and become sufficiently important to hold markets and practice a diversity of trades around the minor port near the mouth of the River Meon.

Land sales increased and peasant holdings were subdivided into smaller plots. Many were however vulnerable to poor harvests with a high mortality level as a consequence and the average holding per family was reported as a mere two acres. This was considerably less than the ten acres considered to be the minimum requirement to support a peasant family at subsistence level.

The Abbey came to an end when Henry VIII persuaded his Council to pass an Act dissolving all the religious houses. He appropriated the enormous estates for his own purposes and much of the spoils were passed to his friends and servants.

As a consequence the Abbey was converted to a stately home in 1537. As Place House it became the home of Thomas Wriothesley, later to be first Earl of Southampton. The new mansion was the centre of some 5000 acres which made Wriothesley one of the two largest landowners in Hampshire at the time. He also came to acquire Beaulieu and Quarr on the Isle of Wight at the same time.

His successor the third Earl of Southampton, Shakespeare's patron, worked hard to exploit the land resources. For the purpose he reclaim large stretches of marshland, now Titchfield Haven, near the mouth o the River Meon, causing a sea-wall to be built. This momentous event was described by the parish register as the 'shutting out of Titchfield haven by one Richard Talbotte's industrie under God's permissione' an has been marked ever since by the Bonfire Boys' Carnival which originated from the ceremonial burning of the Earl's effigy by disaffected villagers.

After the Civil War of 1642-46 the extensive estates in the region we owned by Edward, Earl of Gainsborough, and the area reflected traditional rural life with evidence of continuing agricultural activity provided by the fifteenth-century tithe barn at Titchfield.

The term "squatting" came into use and was a question of boundari and possessions. There was an unwritten law that if a man could bui house, with a chimney and fireplace, and have a fire burning on the hearth between sunset and sunrise, it was his own. If he also had tim to enclose a piece of land for crops, it was also his. To get this done i the given time, he selected his spot, collected the necessary material (keeping them hidden from the authorities), asked his friends to help him, and on a moonlit night, with their assistance, built his house ve roughly and improved on it as time went on.

So the area known as Locks Heath came to be occupied by squatters such as these who built mud huts from which the owners could not evicted.

By the late eighteenth-century our region was served by major fairs

arkets held regularly at Titchfield and these attracted many buyers
d sellers from the surrounding countryside. Unfortunately these fairs
t only attracted the criminal element but the much-feared recruiting
geants from the service garrisons at Portsmouth.

1750 it is known that smuggling was rife along the coastline from
uthampton to Emsworth and Hill Head was reported to be a 'great
uggling place'.

e foundation and development of Locks Heath was still dozens of
rs away as the nineteenth century dawned. Nearby such as
tsmouth and Gosport grew rapidly to reflect the naval and military
vity in the nation.

the low-lying generally flat coastal plain only the odd farm with
tered peasant holdings were dotted around the heathland.

r the centuries the settlements had been in the main dependent on
important medieval market and ecclesiastical centres of Titchfield
its abbey.

form of development in the local area was to be determined during
mid-nineteenth century from an unusual and original source, but
itably with an agricultural base.

NISH BACON

historians tell us that a battle was fought against the Danes in
k Lane. The piece of land where the skirmish was said to have
n place was opposite Cold East Lodge and was named Battle Field
eafter. In their haste to depart the Danes left a boat sunk in the
Hamble, which was still in existence until a few years ago.

A LOCAL PRE-HISTORIC FIND

Evidence of pre-historic activity in the area was the finding of Iron Age
pottery as recent as 1960 at Cumber Copse. The finds are now in
Portsmouth City Museum.

AS WE ARE

When the Vicar Bruce Carpenter wrote in his Foreword to Trevor Cox's
History of Locks Heath produced in 1974 that "There is little doubt that
the year of our centenary in 1994 will see a very different Locks Heath
to the one we now know" he and the locals were awaiting the
publication of the 'South Hampshire Local Plan for Locks Heath and
District' with some trepidation.

Bruce Carpenter knew that a population explosion was to be "planned"
but he could not have envisaged an increase of the order of 10, 000
plus in the next twenty years.

The last twenty years have seen many housing estates and
developments of varying sizes spring up in every gap available and
many have covered what were formerly strawberry fields.

The Locks Heath Centre has been built to meet the retail and
community needs of the area. Much industrial development has
complemented the population growth with sites and units located at
Segensworth. Large retail units of the 'warehouse variety' have been
sited along the A27 road and have attracted large retailers such as
M.F.I., Allied Carpets, B&Q, and Halfords. Commercial radio stations
have also been attracted to the area to site their studios.

AS WE WERE

In the beginning (1866 to be precise)

Its not so long ago that the bustling overgrown village of Locks Heath did not exist. Until about 120 years ago the area was no more than a thousand acres of heathland - a typical 'common' consisting of rough pasture, gorse and broom and a few old oak trees.

When the famous radical journalist William Cobbett made his famous marathon ride across the South of England in the early part of the last century he provided a commentary on each area in his book "Rural Rides". On leaving Fareham and travelling west towards Southampton he recorded - " A large part of the ground is a common enclosed some years ago, it is therefore among the worst of the land in the country".

The only signs of life came from the peasants who eked out a living from the Common by keeping cattle, collecting and selling firewood, cutting turf or fishing in the streams.

Locks Heath has boundaries which are practically identical with those of the old Titchfield Common. The east side of Locks Heath extends from Dimmock's Corner to the Sluice, along Warsash Road, up Raley Road and so roughly covering a triangle.

The area was transformed by the Enclosure Act of 1866 whereby the Common was, like hundreds in the rest of the country, divided up into plots which were then awarded by a Commissioner to those who held land or property in the adjoining parishes. It is reported that the Lords of the Manor involved, a Mr. Hornby and a Mr. Delme-Ratcliffe, had to be compensated for surrendering their rights by the granting of land.

The 1000 acres of the old Titchfield Common were mapped out by the Commissioner and early roads , which had formerly been paths, such Huntspond, Abshot and Lock's were put in. Gates had to be erected to prevent animals straying across the boundaries and two names from those, Hook Gate and Park Gate, are still with us.

On the early maps Hunts Pond Road was no more than a thin pencil line marking a gravel lane. The constant use of ponies and traps on the road ground the gravel into powder which was up to six inches deep. The winter rains clogged the drains and ditches and for weeks the pony or donkey traps struggled through a sea of mud.

The terms 'Heath', 'Common' and 'Moor' were all used by our forefathers to describe areas of common land.

Soon what had been an uncultivated heath was transformed as the gorse and heather was cleared by local men. Large and small plots were claimed and bought from ditch to ditch for agricultural use and the owners were responsible for separating their plots. Hedges of quickthorn and laurel were planted and a patchwork of fields of varying shapes and sizes was evident.

A new network of roads appeared at the turn of the century and a significant number of properties were constructed of which many were of solid brick construction and a marked improvement on the small crowded labourer's cottages to be found in nearby Titchfield which are now so sought after in today's property market for their "character"

Myrtle Worthington, age 3, with her father Joseph at their Locks Road smallholding (c. 1928). Myrtle and her husband Charlie Horne have recently celebrated their golden wedding anniversary

"STRAWBERRY FIELDS FOREVER"

It was a farmer from Curdridge about six miles away who had taken a plot locally who realised the strawberry-growing potential of Locks Heath which led to the one unifying feature in the Parish's short history. It was Louis Lynn who almost single-handedly put Locks Heath on the map and played a part in the establishment of our St. John's Church a few years later.

Lynn bought land from Dimmock's Corner to Abshot Road including the Windmill Farm in Hunts Pond Road and he began to grow the famous Joseph Paxton strawberries on a large scale. About 1884 Lynn moved to Locks Heath with his first farm at the Highlands Farm estate in Locks Road. His second farm could be found at Lock's Farm in the same road and later his third at The Windmill Farm in Hunts Pond Road. It was not long before Locks Heath was established as the major strawberry-growing area in the country. The virgin soil, with good drainage from the sand and gravel under-soil, produced ideal conditions for abundant growth, coupled with the southern climate.

The proud possessor of each plot looked for a crop that would give them the quickest return for their outlay and labour. The strawberry grew well locally and provided an early market sale such that given a reasonable crop an acre or two could provide a good living for a family when labourer's wages were less than 20/- per week.

The story is that it was every young labourer's ambition to become his own master by acquiring an acre or two of strawberry land. Many men started off in this manner by purchasing cheap land with a little capital and went on to become considerable owners of property and wealth as a consequence.

Later Servicemen returning from the Great War bought small plots of land and it became apparent that a mere two or three acres of strawberries would earn sufficient to support a family for the whole of the year.

Wagons carrying supplies of manure to enrich the stony soil and water-carts to supply water to the fields were common sights. The local growers produced tons of strawberries from acres of productive fields and smallholdings which had to be transported by pony or donkey traps down gravel roads to the nearby Botley Railway Station for despatch daily to all parts of the country.

The Swanwick Railway was completed in 1888 and had to cope with queues of carts waiting to have their baskets of strawberries loaded on to the wagons. Its reported that at the peak of the trade 3000 tons of strawberries were loaded at Swanwick and that took no account of the growers who took their produce to Fareham and Botley Stations to avoid the long waits in the queues. It was recorded by some means that in the 1928 season 1,287,925 baskets left Swanwick Station for London to take advantage of the lucrative markets there. Much of the crop was grown for the London market, whose salesmen spoke highly of the local fruit, and the story is that up to sixty pair-horse wagons were needed to convey the fruit from Waterloo to the markets.

We know from photographs that around Swanwick Station queues of carts stretched back as far as Raffo's Garage, all waiting for many hours to unload. The Swanwick Fruit Growers' Association grew up around the station and at the turn of the century they were able to negotiate improved carrying terms with the railway companies and realise better prices at the big markets. The cross-handled wicker baskets, usually holding about six pounds, had covers overprinted with the name of the wholesaler and were packed on to the trains by small boys earning three-pence an hour squeezing into the narrow spaces between the shelves in the goods-wagons.

Wagons drawn by a pair of heavy horses carried the produce and set in the early hours for Portsmouth and Southampton to arrive at the shops and markets before opening time. Certainly the prosperity of Locks Heath, and subsequently Warsash, Botley and Sarisbury as the industry expanded, in its first thirty years or so centred around the frenzied activity in those six or seven weeks in and around the strawberry fields. Apart from the nearby Bursledon brickworks the strawberries were virtually the sole source of employment for the local folk.

To harvest the large quantities of fruit produced a tremendous labour resource was necessary and this problem was overcome by the importing of large numbers of itinerant workers for the season. Travelling people and gipsies invaded the area at harvest-time with their horses, carts and tents, and the inevitable dogs, and Locks Heath was temporarily transformed. The itinerants were known as "Joe pickers' after the best known variety "Sir Joseph Paxton". Their coming was heralded by a cacophony of noise and horse-drawn, brightly-painted caravans, livestock, tents or "benders" (ribs of wood bent to a semi-circle and covered by tarpaulin or sacks) soon became a part of the scenery. Many of the itinerant workers worked for the same grower many years and then eventually settled in the area. It was common for them to take up growing in their own right, to find their own home and put down roots of further generations.

On arrival for the season, usually after horse-trading at the nearby Wickham Fair on May 21st, the menfolk would busy themselves in "strawing-down", which involved putting down the straw around the plants to prevent the berries from touching the soil. Their womenfo

uld be out in the area, often with their infants, covering many miles
h their baskets hawking clothes-pegs or flowers. When picking
an the family would come together in the fields and usually retire to
pub in the evening. The area had a "lively night-life" i.e. there were
quent pub fights with the women-folk highly vocal in their
ouragement of their men-folk. Fights out in the fields were
ctacles for the locals.

of the ready supply of the fruit grew a jam factory opened by Lynn
unts Pond Road and the sweet smell of the fruit filled the air for
se few vital weeks of production. The venture was not a success and
factory became Locks Heath Laundry in 1922.

aging and marketing techniques had to be refined over the years
the earliest type of container used was the wicker basket known as
"Hampshire Gallon". These were mainly made by prisoners in
chester Jail and it was common to see mountains of these baskets
d high on the roadside approaches to Swanwick Station. Eventually
dard baskets of two sizes 2lb and 4lb were introduced made from
woven strips of wooden bands, cut to a very thin section from
orted poplars. A carrying handle of the same material was attached
the whole thing secured by staples.

tably baskets were in themselves big business and produced by the
sand to that local design by a factory in Windmill Farm.

was brought from Titchfield after much difficulty piping it up Coach
As a result it was possible to have a ten horse-power gas engine to
ate three stitching and three saw benches through numerous
ys to make the wood-veneer baskets and power-drive the stapling
hine. The factory existed until the early fifties employing as many as
ocal people, usually girls, all year round to produce sufficient

baskets for the picking time.

In addition the Swanwick and District Basket Factory was established in
1913 adjacent to the railway station. The factory was run as a co-
operative, under the chairmanship of Mr. H.A.D. Dimmick initially, and
adapted and shaped its designs over the years finally producing the
light and attractive plastic punnets.

A successful season was critical for Locks Heath's basic industry and at
propitious moments during the growing period prayers were offered for
fair weather and a healthy crop. During the season the picking started
as early as 4 a.m. for the 10 a.m. trains to such as Aberdeen, Glasgow
and Dublin, after the teams of women and children had walked to the
fields in Locks Heath and Fleet End. Those children who were too young
to work were taken in by the local gentry and entertained royally with
team and games. The back-breaking work continued through the day
to supply the nearer markets of Covent Garden and Brentford, before
the relief of a few snatched hours of sleep in the homes, camps or
caravans and then dawn broke again. The local school holidays were
organised to coincide with the harvesting from mid-June to mid-July.

It is told that the local celebrations for the Coronations of both Edward
VII and George V were postponed until all the berries had been
gathered in.

It was the custom for a glass of beer to be handed round after a certain
number of baskets (say 1000) had been picked. It was clearly thirsty
work and it was reported that the off-licence at Park Gate had a
standing order to supply a firkin of beer (about nine gallons) every day
to each of the fields throughout the season.

The strawberry picking had many spin-offs for the area , not least of which were the sand and gravel pits operating to maintain and widen the web of pony and cart tracks, with the largest extractions in the Chilling and Hook areas.

The decline of the industry started in the 1930s and the boom years for stawberries were all but over, largely because the exhausted earth would no longer yield the crops.

As the industry declined and over the years there was inevitably a transformation in the methods used to cultivate and force the berry. Mechanical devices and weed and pest controls by various scientific methods were introduced. Crop protection was unknown to the pre-1914 growers but soon intense competition from French strawberries grown outside under glass forced the locals here to pioneer this method and adopt a cloche culture.

The Depression, late frosts in 1938 and finally the outbreak of war hastened the decline of the industry in the thirties. Throughout the post-war period there was a further fall in the acreage given over to the berries as rocketing production costs and competition from Europe took their toll but even today there are professional growers in the area who maintain the tradition. By the 1940s the trend was towards general produce - anemones, tomatoes, mushrooms, chrysanthemums, bulbs and ferns - cultivated under glass. Even lettuces which would fit between the young strawberry runners became a popular crop.

1949 was a particularly bad year for the specialist strawberry growers as they fought the temperamental earth for a living. Nurseries were springing up all round the district with vast areas under glass. "Locks Heath Nurseries" under the proprietorship of Mr. Frank Holmes boasted the largest greenhouse in Hampshire given over to the cultivation of tomatoes. Imported produce was at that time subject to tariffs so

foreign competition had been virtually extinguished and the home producers in our area had a huge market at their disposal.

Looking back however it is clear that in those forty boom years or so from the 1870s Locks Heath had been established and it was all down to those sumptuous berries and Mr.Louis Lynn's initiative and foresight. Now strawberries are almost a minor diversion and associated with the recent phenomenon of "pick your own".

That seasonal excitement and frenzied activity which engulfed every citizen of Locks Heath, both young and old, every year are long since over.

Carts loading the berries at Swanwick Station

LOCK'S HEATH - AN 1895 DIRECTORY

PRIVATE RESIDENTS

Rev. Thomas Archer Meynell ARCHER-SHEPHERD - Vicarage

Ralph BURTON - Westward House

James CLARK

David DAVIS - Osborne Villa

William GREEN - Highlands

The Misses HORSFALL - Locksley

John Isaac JONES - Park Gate Road

Charles KELLER - Copse Hill

Francis KELLER - The Limes

Richard LANE - Rose Bank

Mrs. LUKIN - Brookheath

Louis LYNN - Brookheath

Mrs. MAY - Waights Town

Richard Combe MILLER - Oaksleigh Cottage

Isaac MOTT - Park Gate

Mrs. Sylvester - Park Lodge

COMMERCIAL

John BURTON, fruit grower, Park Gate.

Charles CHASE, fruit grower, Abshot Road.

James CLARK, fruit grower.

William COLLIS, boot maker, Park Gate

Henry COX, fruit grower, Warsash Road.

Chas. CROCKFORD, market gardener, Brook Lane.

Edmund DIBBENS, strawberry grower, Park Gate.

Bennett EEDY, fruit grower, Camiola.

George FORD junior, fruit grower, Locks Road

George FORD, market gardener, Locks Road.

William FREEMANTLE, fruit grower, Battlefield.

George GEORGE, fruit grower, Abshot Road.

George GODDARD, fruit grower, Common.

Uriah GODDARD, shopkeeper, farmer and post-office, Park Gate.

James GODDEN, market gardener, Abshot Road.

Philip HARDING, market gardener.

Richard HARFIELD, market gardener, Common.

Caleb HEATH, fruit grower, Brook Lane.

James HEIN, jam manufacturer.

Charles KELLER, fruit grower.

George KENT, market gardener, Locks Road.

Miss Esther KING, dress maker, Park Gate.

Henry KING, fruit grower, Abshot Road.

Solomon LOCK, market gardener, Locks Road.

George MAY, fruit grower, Park Gate.

John MOODY, builder.

Thomas MORLEY, fruit grower.

William MOSLEY, fruit grower, Warsash Road.

William OLDEN, fruit grower.

Thomas ORCHARD, fruit grower, Park Gate.

Philip PEAGRAM, market gardener, Brook Lane.

Charles PEARCE, fruit grower, Warsash Road.

John PLUMBLEY, fruit grower, Abshot Road.

Edgar SMITH, fruit grower.

Robert STUBBS, market gardener, Beacon Bottom.

George THOMPSON, market gardener.

Mrs. TOMKINS, market gardener, Common.

Albert TOULSON, farmer, Brook Farm.

George TROWBRIDGE, fruit grower, Hunts Pond Road.

Henry WAIGHT, fruit grower, Waight's Turning.

William WAIGHT, fruit grower, Abshot Road.

Charles WEST, fruit grower, Locks Road.

George WILKINS, fruit grower, Brook Lane.

Mrs. Mary WILLIAMS, fruit grower, West View.

Hunts Pond Road at the turn of the century

STRAWBERRIES FIT FOR A KING

By 1872 it was Hampshire, and in particular the growing centres of Swanwick, Botley, Sarisbury and Locks Heath, who were providing the earliest outdoor strawberries for the public market.

Many strawberries found their way to Covent Garden for the "London season" which King Edward V11 and his high-born lady friends had done much to establish. The social scene and its attendant functions must have been popular with the local Locks Heath growers. Strawberries with sugar and cream were on the menus at Ascot, Lord's, Henley and Wimbledon, not to mention The Ritz and the fashionable Lyons Tea Houses.

The fruit from our area was known in the trade as "Southamptons" and was soon recognised nationally as being of superior quality to that obtained from cultivation by competitors in Cornwall.

Foreign competition was always a factor and particularly from France. In June 1913 the "Hampshire Independent" reported that local growers were suffering from competition from a French strawberry grown under glass. Not under glasshouses but with glass laid along the rows.

The newspaper reported however that "the view of the connoisseur is that the outdoor variety is invariably superior to the forced variety, and the result was that when the first berries reached Covent Garden from Hampshire they fetched a price far in advance of that which the French growers had been receiving."

The berries were rushed to the London markets by early-morning trains and fleets of trucks. The best known fleet was operated by "W. Waight", the owner being Wally Waight.

The first variety grown in the area was known as the "Maud" and was on the small side, about the size of a thimble and in great contrast to the huge luscious strawberry cultivated in recent years.

Later came the "Joey" or "Paxtons", short for "Sir Joseph Paxton" the producer of this strain, and much larger than the "Maud", and considered by many experts to be the most delicious berry ever grown. Described as of rich crimson colour it was of a good and uniform shape. "The Royal Sovereign" became a very popular strain and had its own ardent supporters. Other varieties to be developed included "Merton Princess", "Laxton", "Bedford Champion" and "Madame Kooi", the latter from Holland. A variety called "Noble" had its supporters with its large round berry but less flavour.

It was in 1913 that a new variety was introduced which was to be prov disastrous to the growers. The "Madame La Fevebre" (also known as "Lady Lefebvre") was favoured and was for several years known as a good cropper. However it appears that this variety brought the deadly disease known as root rot to the area. Crops were badly hit as a consequence and this coupled with the Depression led to many growe going bankrupt. Those who survived were further hit by the severe fros in 1938 and then by the War.

Hundreds of ruddy-faced gipsies or travellers invaded the area as picke for the picking rate of a penny farthing per four-pound chip basket or pence per hour. Whole families would work up to eighteen hours per Children on leave from school would walk three or four miles from ho in Titchfield or Botley to start work at say Fleet End at four in the morning. Finishing at ten in the evening they would make the walk ho again.

The strawberries were at first exported in seven-pound wicker baskets made in Winchester prison. With the addition of 'pound punnets' it m

...ound of fruit a very acceptable size to consumers.

...a type the area's growers were shrewd, often hard-headed, business-...n and not, as subsequent generations might imagine, just simple ...untry folk. Strawberry growing was an industry which demanded ...ous commercial judgements and, like market gardening today, good ...paration, organisation and management. It was reported however that ...greed of some of the growers dealt a severe blow to the trade in that ...quantities in the baskets were systematically lessened. The practice ...s identitifed when some baskets were sent to market and found to ...tain 6oz. or less of fruit.

...a consequence the traders were for some time wary of buying ...uthamptons". In the event the 'handle basket' was introduced and ...se could generally be relied on to contain exactly 6lb of strawberries. ...en however growers did not learn from the previous experience and in ...face of narrow margins were tempted to give short measure, to the ...eral dissatisfaction of the public and the injury of the trade. In the ...n however this practice had to be abandoned in the face of fierce ...lity from the trade and the baskets of "Southamptons" could be ...d upon to contain the full measure.

...m factory was started in the early years of the century by Louis Lynn ...company called Lynn, Hoare & Co. with many local residents as ...eholders. The venture was only moderately successful and the ...ings were taken over by Army and Navy Stores upon the demise of ...ousiness. Eventually the premises were converted to accomodate a ...dry which had started up.

...n the fruit became small towards the end of the season it was picked ...m making and dispatched to various jam factories. Older residents ...f the tricks used by the gipsy pickers to increase the weight of the jam strawberries. Fruit would be brought to a factory in 1/2 cwt. barrels and as they passed a pond would tip a bucket of water into the barrel. When the workers at the factory came to empty the barrels they found tadpoles and bits of weed in them after the water and berries had been removed. Other pickers put stones in the bottom of the barrels to bring the weight up.

Stable manure was extensively used as fertiliser on the beds, although phosphates were occasionally used as a chemical fertiliser. Before the use of motor transport the horse manure was obtained from the Nine Elms Stables of the old London and South Western Railway. It was delivered in rail trucks to Swanwick station and from there carted by the growers and paid for by the ton.

After the fruit season the growers had to rake up the bedding straw which was usually burned. Then the rows had to be weeded by hand and later runners were laid from the existing plants to provide new ones.

The rest of the year was taken up with ploughing, digging and manuring the beds, along with planting new plants about November time.

The W. Waight fleet

LOUIS LYNN (1850-1921)

A pioneer strawberry-grower and churchman

Louis Lynn was born on 12 January 1850, the son of a shepherd, at Albury in Surrey, between Guildford and Dorking. He was the second of five children of Louis and Lucy Lynn.

It is suggested that Louis Lynn senior was employed by the Shrine family who owned a number of farms in the south of England. When the last of the Shrine family passed away it is mooted that the farms were left to their various shepherds including Lynn senior. Lynn senior may have inherited the farm at Curdridge and passed it to his son to run.

By the age of 23 Lynn had acquired sufficient means from this farming to buy land at Egham and build two detached houses for occupation by the Lynn and Tickner families.

By the time of the 1881 Census Lynn was shown as farming Wangfield Farm (145 acres) at Curdridge in Hampshire and by the time of his death in 1921 he had become the second largest local landowner, surpassed only by Quintin Hogg whose Holly Hill estate took in the whole of Warsash and Locks Heath as far as Locks Road.

Whilst at Curdridge Lynn had formed a close friendship with the large intellectual Lukin family. When he moved to Locks Heath to realise the enormous potential for strawberry-growing Lynn seems to have shared houses with both Mrs. Joanna Bryan Lukin, at "Brookheath" until her death at the age of 92 in 1894, and then her daughter Mary Pauline Lukin until her subsequent death at the age of 67 in 1897. His liasions with such prestigious clerical families as the Lukins, and later the Skrines, were reflections of Lynn's intense religious interests.

There was no place to worship in the vicinity so Lynn, encouraged by the Lukins, held religious meetings at Windmill Farm in Hunts Pond Road initially. When St. Johns Mission Church was built in 1886 Lynn was the driving force and inspiration behind the effort and the raising of the necessary funds.

Lynn played a full part in the early life of St. Johns being the very first churchwarden and as a layman regularly took charge of the 'Children's service' held at 11 a.m. at the Mission.

Lynn bought great slices of land from Dimmocks Corner to Abshot Road to include the Windmill Farm in Hunts Pond Road and he began to grow strawberries on a large scale. In addition his vast orchards growing such as damsons and Bramley apples provided much employment. Later Lynn opened a jam factory in the same road to capitalise on the supply of the quantities of fruit.

Lynn sold two plots in Hunts Pond Road , one to a Mr. Hicks who then gave the land for the building of a Congregational Chapel in 1902 and the other on the corner to a Mr. 'Inky' Cox who had a shop built in 19 which is now 'Dimmocks'.

Lynn was probably the first to bring golf to the village when he set aside two acres in the Second Park. He would play there with his friends, one whom was Mr. Stoner of Cuthberts Road who bred the famous strain 'Money Maker' tomatoes.

Lynn's influence was such that when he frowned upon the opening of further shops in the area the Locks Heath residents were forced to rely street traders with ponies and traps from Fleet End and Warsash.

Miss Ellen Maria Skrine died in 1894 at the age of 68 and was buried Hook cemetery. Lynn's close relationship with her was such that he sha

grave on his death 27 years later and in her will she described Lynn as
r adopted son".

n variously occupied properties at "Brookheath", "Locksheath House"
903 and "Highlands" in 1907, passing away at the latter in 1921. The
estate at the "Highlands" was made available by Lynn as a venue for
n-air meetings, fairs and fetes of the Women's Institute, St. John's
rch and the Chapel. On his death the following properties and estates
ether with cottages, farm buildings, orchard and plots of fruit land
ned part of his estate to be sold - "Highlands", "Southleigh",
kdene", "Locksheath Park Estate" and "Fleetlands".

ay's Locks Heath Shopping Centre was built on the site of one of the
ards on Lynn's "Highlands" farm estate. Surprisingly there is no
tion of Lynn in the Centre or indeed in any road names in the district.

Sale on Lynn's death included valuable fixed basket-making
ninery and the Letters Patent obtained by Lynn in 1915 for his
ntion related to the 'construction of non-returnable boxes or baskets
ne carriage of fruit'. The specification provided that 'such boxes or
ets could be readily built up or constructed on the spot by the fruit
ver and by the aid of unskilled labour e.g. child or female labour'.

's will ensured that most of his bequests were to clerics and their
ies, including Rev. John Harcourt Skrine and Rev. James Lukin. As a
tion of his close association with the Lukin family the executors of
s estate were named as Major Tudor-Craig and Theophilus Brown,
of whom had married into the family.

s father, still a shepherd, died in 1914 but had not merited a
ion in his son's copious will.

any years Lynn was a conspicuous figure as he travelled the area,

usually sporting a large cream-coloured Panama hat, driving a pony and
trap. To the locals he was "Joey Lynn", nicknamed after the Joseph
Paxton strawberries he grew in such profusion.

Not one picture appears to exist of Lynn or his associates and this is a
disappointment to Mr. Lewis Read, of Shepperton in Middlesex, who has
been researching the life of his great-uncle for some years.

An old postcard from 1913 is the nearest he has got to a picture. The
postcard shows the old aeroplane which had made an emergency landing
on part of his land. Lynn and his companions are in the distant
background with a pony and trap but the figures cannot really be
identified.

Lynn had been a hugely influential figure in the founding not only of
Locks Heath itself but also of St. John's Church. His influence in putting
the area's land to such a unique and valuable purpose could be felt for so
many years. By his pioneering work in pointing the way initially to a
Mission Church for the area and by being one of the inspirations behind
the building of St. John's Church Lynn has a special place in the centenary.

The carts queue to await unloading at the station

"THE TIMES" 29 APRIL 1938

'Early strawberries record broken in spite of drought'

A report from the 'The Times Own Correspondent' described a record in Locks Heath when fruit was sent to the London markets in April. Mr. E.W. Edwards, secretary of the local fruit growers' association, commented - "It is the first time within living memory that we have started picking in April".

The strawberries were grown naturally under cloches and not forced and made from three to five shillings a pound. All this was in spite of an absence of rain since the middle of January and the prevalence of north-east winds which had the effect of drying the soil rapidly. It was reported by "The Times" as the 'longest and severest drought ever known in the district'.

AN OLD WIVES' TALE

At a local spot called "Three Stone Bottom" there was concern about the movement of the stones for no reason. It was said that one could pick three stones from the stream and say "When they hear Titchfield Church clock strike twelve at midnight they will turn over". At this the three stones were supposed to cross the road to the other side on the stoke of midnight.

Nearby was a dyke where tramps and travellers would stop for water. Some said that that the tramps regularly arranged them in such a way as to give a signal to their fellow travellers so that on their arrival they would know of their earlier movements.

SIR JOSEPH PAXTON

The producer of the strain of strawberry know as the "Joey", Sir Josep Paxton, started as a gardener's boy and developed a keen interest in horticulture. He was a head gardener at the estate of the Duke of Northumberland but it was during his employment at Chatsworth Gardens subseqently that his employer the sixth Duke of Devonshire noticed his "general air of alertness".

During his thirty years at Chatsworth he became head gardener, esta agent and house steward. He did the Duke's business with lawyers, travelled with him abroad, dined as a friend at the Duke's table, not mention marrying the housekeeper's niece, Sarah Brown.

Joe was also a railway pioneer, built a big country house for a corps navvies in the Crimean War, and presided over a House of Commons Committee which planned the Thames Embankment.

His best known botanical triumph was with a water-lily called Victori Regia. This new lily had refused to flower at Kew but in 1849 Paxton obtained a plant for Chatsworth, designed and built a special greenhouse and tank for it , and succeeded in making it flower.

It was the Great Exhibition of 1851 which brought his greatest trium however. Paxton put his great knowledge of glasshouses to good us designing and constructing the great glass building in Hyde Park kno as "The Crystal Palace". There were reportedly 233 architects and builders with rival schemes but it was Paxton who won the approval the Committee and subsequently the public with his design. After th exhibition of the wonders of the industrial age the whole thing was removed to Sydenham for permanent display.

e area known as Winnards Copse in Warsash comprised an 80-acre
odland estate owned by aristocracy and was also the site of a
autiful country home. It was Sir Joseph Paxton who was
mmissioned to landscape the whole of the estate for the owners.

en two farm cottages were converted into a hotel, later to become
inn/public house, for the growing population of Locks Heath it was
med after the gentleman who had given his name to his own
wberry, and also had more claim to fame than that.

The "Sir Joseph Paxton" in its early days as an hotel

WHAT'S IN A NAME?

Locks Heath

We know that a small farm dating from Tudor times was in the
ownership of a yeoman farmer called Lock. This is generally accepted to
be the same James Lock, who with his wife Ruth, is buried in a grave to
be found in the St. Peter's Titchfield church yard. The gravestone shows
Lock to have lived from 1780-1817 and he is reckoned to have acquired
the land for his farm through an association with the Earl of
Southampton. The farm became known as Lock's Farm and as its size
grew it was a prominent feature of the heath. If you crossed the heath
by the footpath you would pass close to the farm with its duck pond
and giant yew tree. It was common for the monks from nearby
Titchfield Abbey to pass the farm on their way to their fish pond in the
neighbouring village of Hook.

Much later a rough road called Peters Road led across the common to
Lock's Farm. For most of this century the farm house in Locks Road was
occupied by the Godfrey family and in particular by the sisters of that
name. Now the house is owned by the Abbeyfield Society as one of
their homes and known as 'The Stables'.

Inevitably that part of the common occupied by the farm became
known to the passing monks as Lock's Heath. Other travellers would
cross the common after having passed through one of the gates, some
of the names of which have survived viz. Park Gate, Hook Gate and
Common Gate.

A pound for horses was at Common Gate and it was one of the duties
of the warden of the common to round up the horses for branding. The

"commoners" were permitted to graze their cattle at will. They could claim the land which they had enclosed if they were able to build a house of mud and have a fire alight by the following morning. Even in those days such occupants were known as "squatters".

Smuggling from the coast was rife and hiding places on the heathland were found for the contraband, the entrances for which were guarded by fearsome dogs. Tales of ghosts, black dogs and other fearsome things were spread to keep people indoors at night and leave the way clear for the smugglers.

On the 1880 edition of the local ordnance survey covering the Titchfield parish Locks Road is identified as a carriage-way rather than an unnamed farm track. The locality is referred to as Locks Heath and Locks Farm is shown. On the site of the present Shopping Centre Locks Heath Farm can be found.

At the time of the 1860 Enclosure Acts the cartographers had to put names to districts and features and it is reasonable to assume that they would turn to the name of such an existing property as Lock's Farm as a base. Later in the 1890s the name of the property was changed by the residents to "Highlands", possibly by the Lukins.

There has in the past been some conjecture as to whether the farms were in fact at a later date in the ownership of another Mr. James Lock who was known to be a most successful businessman and entrepreneur from Warsash. One wonders whether he was in fact a descendant of the earlier James Lock.

This particular Mr. Lock had originally in the early 1850s been a rag and bone gatherer before turning to selling fish and meat near the shore at Warsash. His fortunes improved considerably when he acquired several vessels and built up a thriving business by dealing in crabs and shellfish. It was said that he made use of the old fishponds in the Lock's Farm area to keep the fish alive until they were required for sale.

If this connection has validity then it is interesting to contemplate that our thriving area of Locks Heath may have been named after a rag and bone man.

Part of the original Lock's Farm

ory is that at the lower end of the gravel track was a pit which
led with water and formed a pond. It is said that an unfortunate
alled Hunt fell into the pond and drowned. The subsequent road
appears to commemorate this sad event in the area's history.

ad followed the old common boundary all the way up to Park
going from a stream called the Sluice, at the Titchfield end, over
were two culverts. One was installed in the very early days, and
cond after the common was enclosed. The tracks from which
ld roads were made were not originally straight. Only when the
were made up finally were they straightened up.

n the last century plots of land were apportioned by the Titchfield
as "allotments for ever" for the use of householders of the parish
e properties lacked sufficient ground for a garden. The plots are of
e still put to very good use to this day.

ad originally was made up of gravel, with countless stones which
o be regularly raked off otherwise the passing carts were liable not
o have a rough ride but to be tipped over.

rst fifty years of this century are perceived to be made up of clearly
ed seasons with hot summers and extremely wet winters. Hunts
Road reflected this with the nuisance from dust on the dry gravel
n summer and flooding in the winter.

ain-water swept down the road, filled the ditches and created
nous ponds. The biggest expanse of water could be found at the
field end (where the road now meets the Warsash Road) where the
ant pond made it difficult for the monks from the Abbey to pass

through to their fishing ponds further on.

The road was distinguished by its lining of oak trees from one end to
the other, many of which have been pulled down as the road has
developed. .

The first cottage in the road at the Titchfield end was one of four
lodges at each corner of the estate attached to Hotham House, (now
West Hill School), owned by Lord Hotham. The other lodges, (North,
South and East), housed such as maids, gardeners and coachmen, but
the West Lodge was the home of the butler.

The road originally extended along open common land until the
growers built what were predictably called "strawberry houses" and the
common was broken up into patches and purchased for fruit growing.
Many of the houses were built by soldiers returning from the Boer War
and this is reflected in the house names which remain to this day e.g.
"Louisville" and "Ladysmith". The Managing Director of the Jam
Factory, appointed by the owner Louis Lynn, occupied the latter
property after his war service.

Older residents remember that as children they would play marbles in
the rough road on their way home from the village's mixed school. One
resident recalls that Hunts Pond Road was a popular route for funeral
hearses to and from burials at Titchfield or Sarisbury and that she
secured many a lift home from school sitting on the back of the empty
vehicles.

As well as countless strawberry plots Hunts Pond Road was the site for
the jam factory, founded by Louis Lynn, in the early part of the century.
For residents in the road the jam factory was well known to them as the
source of a ghastly smell. With no proper drainage in place a frothy

residue passed out from the processes into the open ditches of Hunts Pond Road and Cyprus Lane and was dispersed into the open fields whilst emitting a foul stench.

Subsequently the laundry on the site of the jam factory was best remembered for a loud whistle which reportedly could be heard for miles around when it was sounded to mark the lunch break at noon for the staff and again one hour later as call to return to work.

In the road in the early days could also be found the Pound House within which any strays from herds of cattle passing through the district were kept after being rounded up. It was then up to the farmers to visit the house on a regular basis to claim any of their animals.

Admiral's Road

The name derives from Admiral Maxey who lived in Holly Hill, Sarisbury and who owned some land in Lock's Road.

Peters Road

Mr. Quintin Hogg came to live in the district at Holly Hill House and was accompanied by a Mr. Peters who was a prominent strawberry-grower.

Pest House

At Number 347 Hunts Pond Road can be found a two-storey red brick house of distinction which was in fact built more than one hundred years ago as a pox hospital.

It is said that a grandmother was collecting winkles at Brownwich shore when she was infected with smallpox by a smuggler. She had to be isolated at the house as a typical early patient of the hospital. For t[...] residents the house was forever known as the "Pest House".

Later the house cum hospital was occupied by overflow patients fr[...] Knowle Hospital who needed to be in isolation whilst being treate[...] various diseases. The house was particularly useful for that purpose during "Asian flu" and diphtheria epidemics. After that the proper[...] became the Gamekeeper's House for many years and occupied by [...] well-known brothers called Ford.

Older residents remember that the pair specialised in putting down disposing of local dogs by request and as a consequence the groun[...] the house are reputed to be filled with their bones.

The house was derelict by 1955 at which time it was converted an[...] modernised for use as a residence under the control of the Earl of Southampton Charity based at Titchfield.

The Earl's Charity Rest Home - formally the Pest House

smond Corner

mond Grove was established through the development of the former unds of the house called 'Jesmond' in Locks Road, and the trees n the original surrounds have been retained.

mmock's Corner

many years there were only two shops in Locks Heath. mmock's", was run by two generations of the family on the her of Hunts Pond Road and Church Road. "Bachelor's" was the l post office on the site of the current occupant "The Fruit and ver Basket".

property on the site was originally built by George "Inky" Cox in 8 but it was in 1925 that Bill and Connie Dimmock took over the eral store. In their advertisement they were described as "Grocer, acconist, general dealer, and confectioner" and this encompassed a goods as diverse as leather goods, biscuits, tools, cigarettes and ets as well as the supply of coal, oil, paraffin and vinegar.

corner where "Dimmock's" was located was originally called Church her but came to be named after the store at the time when buses came to Locks Heath. It was the site of the main bus stop and the e became well-known to the bus conductors and passengers alike as illager parcel collection-point.

illager went to Fareham for a purchase then the usual arrangement for the goods to be taken from the bus-station and delivered to mmock's" by bus for collection subsequently

For the youngsters the major attraction on the corner was the prominent billboard which displayed the posters for the films which were due to be shown in Fareham at the Alexander's Cinema (later known as the Savoy).

In recent years the store on the corner has been converted to an off-licence but at the time of writing is awaiting disposal for another use.

"Doctors Corner"

Locals named this corner of Locks Road and Heath Road after the doctors who lived in the big house located there called "Lockerly". The late Doctor John Kingdon and his father before him were well-known residents from 1923 onwards and they had been preceded by Doctor Wilkins in 1911. The Kingdons were staunch supporters of St. John's and in particular Miss Kingdon who recently passed away. She had lived in the house for many years with her mother.

Doctor Kingdon was a very familiar figure in the area through the 1920s and 30s driving his black Austin Seven motor-car and lent his support to the local football team by agreeing to become their president.

Abshot House

Abshot House was known as the home of the Bradshaw family. Mrs. Augustine Bradshaw's generous contribution to the building of St. Johns Church was marked by her being invited to lay the foundation stone in 1895. Mrs. Bradshaw was the sister of General Gordon of Kharthoum and the family were recognised as very philanthropic as far as local charities and causes were concerned.

Home Rule Road

It is said that this road was originally a pathway and many of the properties therein were occupied by Irish labourers employed in the construction of the railway in the Swanwick district. Apparently when two of their countrymen of managerial status set up home there and had the road built it was named by them in recognition of the home rule granted to their native land.

James Grieve Grove

The land which was given up and sold for development was for many years covered with orchards. The close takes its name from the most common variety of apple which was harvested on the site.

Oaklands Way

This road is on the site of the big house called "Oaklands" where the Jewell family lived for many years and maintained a large strawberry holding.

St. Cuthberts Lane

This lane is said to have been the site of an ancient chapel or monument in the middle of the original Common. This conjecture arose from the discovery of numbers of stones in the vicinity which might have been part of the said religious building. Later the lane lead down to the big house known as 'St. Cuthberts'.

Richards Close

This new road was named in memory of one of the most illustrious figures in Locks Heath's past, Mr. Walter Richards who was not only t Headmaster of the village school for very many years but a prominen and influential figure in both church and local government life.

Lodge Road

Once a narrow lane it led down to the lodge which was situated by gates at the entrance to the drive up to the house known as 'St. Cuthbert's'.

LOCKS HEATH GROWS UP

The main strawberry growing had centred around the Highlands Far Estate in Locks Road, around Locks Farm in the same road, and the Windmill Farm in Hunts Pond Road.

Louis Lynn, the most important grower in the area and the owner o considerable land and property , moved out of his Highland Estate i the last years of the last century to live in the new Brookheath Hous built in the Brook Lane area. Four large houses already existed in the vicinity: Great Brook, Little Brook, Brook Farm and Brook House. The latter was, on its completion, the family home of Quintin Hogg. the original home being at Holly Hill.

These four large houses were all of similar design, based on the firs the area, Brookheath House. The second, built in 1890, in Heath Rc

s Mrs Roxburgh's Southleigh, and the third was in Locks Road, called
arleigh and occupied by a Colonel Wilson. It was reported that in
20 a Colonel Niven took up residence in this latter property with his
alid son. The word is that this was David Niven's uncle and the young
vid visited the house during holidays from boarding-school, before
king his mark in the film world.

fourth house in 1895 was on the corner of Heath Road and Locks
d. Called Lockerly it was occupied by a Doctor Wilkins in 1911 until
retirement when it was acquired by Doctor Kingdon. The spot is still
rred to as "Doctor Kingdon's Corner".

903 Louis Lynn had moved again into Locks Heath House Estate of
acres. The house of his was completely hidden from the road by tall
nd chestnut trees with filbert nut trees lining the carriageways. By
time the imposing Lynn owned the whole of the first and second
Roads, (now St. John's Road and Locks Heath Park Road).

r living in Locks Heath House for four years, until 1907, Lynn moved
into the Highlands, now as the owner until his death.

arsash Road too there were large houses, including Hook Gate,
bury House, Oaklands, The Haven and Jesmond Dean (the latter
re Jesmond Close grew up).

he edge of the parish, beyond Brook Lane, stood the large estate of
Montefiore family known as Cold East, subsequently of course to be
ite of the hospital.

ot House, at the other end of the parish, was the one-time home
e Hornby family who held manorial rights over much of the

Common. The house is of course now the centre of much leisure
activity as a country club. It was from this house that Miss Augusta
Bradshaw, a member of the Hornby family, came to lay the foundation
stone of the new Church of St. John the Baptist in Locks Heath.

The Congregational Church followed in 1902 and the only inn in the
parish, the "Sir Joseph Paxton" named after the eminent Victorian
horticulturist and designer of the Crystal Palace for the 1851 Great
Exhibition in Hyde Park. Thirsts are still slaked in the pub, affectionately
known as "The Joe", to this day.

A Post Office opened, first in Netley Terrace, and later moving to
Dimmock's Corner. Post Offices could also be found in Heath Road and
Park Gate.

The Drill Hall in Bridge Road was erected about 1909 as part of the
nationwide call to arms to counter Germany's increasing military
aspirations and a part-time Territorial Volunteer Army could be found
training there. The force was the 3rd Volunteer Battalion, a detachment
of the Hampshire Regiment.

It was not until 1922 that another hall sprung up known as the Locks
Heath Memorial Hall as a fitting tribute to those sons of the village who
gave their lives in the First World War. In 1956 the Hall passed in the
control of the Fareham Council and its name was changed to the
Community Centre to reflect the range of day and evening activities
carried out under the auspices of a Community Association. In recent
years it has moved back to being known as the Memorial Hall.

CONGREGATIONAL (THEN UNITED REFORMED) CHURCH

A handful of people who met regularly in a private house for prayer meetings, led by Mr. Charles Hicks, were the pioneers of the movement which paved the way for the building of the Locks Heath Congregational Church in 1902. It was Mr. Hicks himself who gave the site to meet the needs of the non-conformist inhabitants of the parish. Mr. Hicks then persuaded Mr. Benjamin Nicholson, a well-known yacht builder - Camper and Nicholson of Gosport - to provide the finance for the project. The church was built entirely by voluntary labour and at completion it was opened in January 1903 with the first service on the 18th of that month.

The church was overseen by the Rev. C.P. Way from Sarisbury Green for the first two years before the Rev. Brewer became the first residing Minister.

The Sunday School started on the opening of the church and this work grew to such an extent that it was necessary in March 1906 to embark on the work of adding a schoolroom to the premises. Mr. Nicholson played his part by promising £50 for every £50 collected by the church towards the cost of almost £800. Unfortunately before this plan could be developed Mr. Nicholson passed away and the church was left to revise their plans.

In the event it was resolved to build the schoolroom by voluntary labour under the leadership of Mr. D. Haynes. As a result of their efforts the foundation stone was laid in November 1907 and the school was opened in the following February.

The work of those resolute voluntary workers did not end there. A cottage next to the church was purchased and when it became vacant extensive additions and alterations were made, and the Manse came into existence.

The debt on the Manse was cleared in 12 years and the next move was to purchase an Army hut nearby which was furnished as a parlour. Youngsters were not forgotten and their "Band of Hope" met weekly. In those early days the teenagers were brought up to go to chapel three times on a Sunday and of course to sign an oath of temperance.

The coming-of-age celebrations included the launching of a fund for new organ and choir pews. The money was raised and in 1925 the organ was dedicated.

Through the generosity of the Misses E. and N. Freemantle electric lighting was installed in the church in 1930 and later they provided acoustic aid for the deaf. Later in 1939 the two sisters provide the greater part of the money needed for the installation of an electric blower for the organ.

At the Golden Jubilee celebrations in 1953 one of the guests was Mrs B. Edwards whose father Mr. Hicks had given the site for the chruch. She was also the first to be married in the church in April 1905.

The Congregational Church in Hunts Pond Road

...and during its demolition

LOCKS HEATH MEMORIAL HALL

The idea of a church hall was first proposed in 1912 by the Winchester Diocese Board of Finance to mark the 21st anniversary of the opening of St. John's Church in 1916. A 'Building Fund' was opened from the time that Mr. Louis Lynn made a gift of the land upon which the hall was to be built. Mr. Lynn had specified in the indenture conveying the land to the Diocesan Board of Finance that a 'Church Memorial Hall' be built.

The original records show that the hall was intended as a parish room for such as church services, young men's club, and other church-related fellowships. Unfortunately Mr. Lynn passed away before he could see the completion of the project.

In the period to the closing of the fund in 1929 the total cost of over £1600 was raised. Of this nearly £1500 was provided by church collections, subscription lists, repayable loans, diocesan grant, and functions organised by church members (including the annual fete), with a little over £100 being received from general subscriptions. One of the most successful events to raise the money was the Church Fete of 1918 which realised £161. The Congregational Church participated in the raising of the £1500 with their own whist drives, fairs, jumble sales etc. Older villagers remember taking pennies from their pocket-money to Sunday School in special envelopes for the fund.

The Great War of 1914-18 held up the project but on its completion a foundation stone was laid by Emmeline Louisa White in November 1921. A Service of Dedication was held on 14 February 1922 by the Bishop of Southampton. Later it was decided by the Parochial Church Council to change the name to a 'Memorial Hall', rather than 'Parish Room' in memory of those who had lost their lives in the parish in the Great War.

It was a condition of the gift of the site that it should be used for "the benefit of the Members of the Church of England in the Parish of Locks Heath". The P.C.C., as Adminstrative Trustees, did not seek to run the Hall on a denominational basis and the Hall Account was always kept separate from Church funds. The Hall was made available for general use in the village on the easiest terms compatible with effective maintenance.

The Hall became the focus for many activities and clubs. At one time the villagers could even view the latest films but such cinema entertainment had to be promptly stopped when it was discovered that the Hall was not licensed for such a purpose. When a license was eventually obtained the non-inflammable type of film had to be used to meet fire regulations. The Hall was the principal meeting place and youngsters in particular were able to join such as the Sunday School, Girls Friendly Society, Band of Hope, and the Boy Scouts. For their elders whist-drives, dances, dramatic shows and concerts satisfied their social needs.

Villagers rarely travelled far outside the parish boundaries with their limited means of transport and budgets. The more adventurous would have an occasional treat with a visit to the cinema at Fareham, Portsmouth or Southampton.

Most amusements were close to home however and outside activities centred around the church, chapel or the village hall.

Many years later in April 1958 a public meeting was held in the Hall to deal with allegations made to the Vicar, Rev. Edwin Curtis, that the

s not strictly a Church building. The feeling had spread in the village
t the building had passed into the hand of the Church Council by
me irregular or discreditable means, when it should have been a
age hall in public ownership.

arge and representative gathering from the church and local
anisations had the history and background to the building fully
lained to them, and the necessary documents as proof were
duced.

he event the true position of the Hall was made clear to the public
the church was reassured that the memorial to the fallen would
tinue to be a centre of goodwill.

he early sixties the cost of the general maintenance and upkeep of
Hall made it unecomonic to run. The rental fees were insufficient as
ling and the rising costs put a particularly heavy burden upon the
rch Council and the congregation. Mr. Louis Lynn's executor had
ed that the Church Council could sell the property if they so wished.
consequence Rev. Edwin Curtis announced that they were
sidering the sale of the hall. The Church Council approached the
ham District to see if it wanted to buy the Hall but initially the
er was the subject of a public meeting, after an outcry in the village
d fears that the Hall might eventually be demolished.

Public Meeting in March 1964 a decision was taken to form a
munity Association and this transpired in July of that year, with the
norial Hall, to be rented, as its centre. Eventually the hall was
sed of to the Fareham Borough Council for use as a Community
re under their control.

A FORCED LANDING

There was great excitement and a crowd gathered when a military
biplane - 'number 269' and known as a 'Gun Bus' - landed in
Locksheath Park on 23 May 1913. It was said that the pilot landed with
a view to calling upon his fiancee, reportedly a Miss Young from Heath
Road. The plane took off the next day but not after finding it difficult to
summon up enough speed in the limited space of the park. Inevitably
the landing attracted a great deal of attention and crowds quickly
gathered in the park, including many children who had dashed up from
the Council School at the bottom of Locks Road.

From one of the photographs of the incident a pony and trap bearing a
gentleman in a familiar panama hat can be spotted prominently among
the crowd - almost certainly it was one Louis Lynn who was a familiar
and respected figure as he travelled the district in that fashion.

After the attention his previous visit had attracted the pilot made his
next visit to this fiancee by landing on the Cold East Estate at Sarisbury.

THE TALL TREES

Monterey pine trees can be sighted on land in the vicinity of the
properties at 109, 113 and 117 Locksheath Park Road.

A California redwood tree together with bay, yew, hornbeam and many
oak trees can be found on land off Locks Road.

A group of trees in the grounds of 118 Locksheath Park Road contain
oak, corsican pine, scots pine, larch, beech and holly.

Lock's Heath Cricket Club 1901.

The laundry girls from Hunts Pond Road

COMMUNICATIONS AND AMENITIES

The opening of Swanwick Railway Station in 1888 was a milestone in that travellers had access to the latest mode of transport and trips to Portsmouth and Southampton did not have to be taken by the laborious farm carts and wagons. Obviously the main benefit was felt initially by the strawberry industry. Otherwise the main form of transport was the pony trap, donkey cart or bicycles with solid tyres.

The first motor car in the area was in the ownership of Doctor Wilkins, the first village doctor having purchased the vehicle in 1911. Otherwise the earliest motor vehicles seen in the area were Army surplus lorries purchased by strawberry carriers after the First World War.

The first bus service in the district started up in 1919 when a Mr. Tutt from Gosport ran a single-decker from Gosport Hard right through to Warsash, and then supplemented this with an ex-London bus.

By the early 1930s services were being run through the area by Provincial, Southdown and Hants and Dorset companies from Portsmouth to both Warsash and Bursledon Bridge.

Our forefathers had access to very few amenities and householders in Locks Heath's early years had their own well with water raised by pump or windlass. In 1894 the South Hants Water Company was permitted to lay mains and supply water so that the locals had their first taste of piped water. Gas came to the area in 1914 from gasworks at Titchfield but in 1951 was replaced by the national grid source. Electricity arrived in 1930 after cables were laid throughout the village - necessarily a tortuous process taking five years in all.

A telephone service was available in the early years of the century through a manual exchange sited in the Locks Heath Post Office in Heath Road. At that time the service was operated by private enterprise and it was reported that there were 171 connections in 1940. When the G. P. took over a new automatic exchange was built in Locks Road in 1947 and since then of course the number of subscribers have increased tremendously and the technology has kept pace with their requirements.

For very many years sewerage was by earth closet in a corner of the garden. This was followed by the cesspit and then the septic tank system which allowed toilets to be placed indoors. The main sewers were laid in the parish as late as the 1960s.

As far as local government was concerned Locks Heath came under the Sarisbury Parish Council until 1932 when the Fareham Urban District Council took over. Ward status was granted in 1950 and now Locks Heath had parity with such as Titchfield, Warsash, and Sarisbury as far elected councillors were concerned.

Initially those councillors, often from the thriving Ratepayers Association represented a quiet country parish with a fairly static population and concerned themselves with nothing more demanding than the provision of street lighting and the deplorable state of unmade roads such as Heath Road, which were often the source of bitter and prolonged complaint.

However the 1960s saw a great change with the population rising from 1000 to 8000, the schools expanding at a fantastic rate and much of it down to large new employers such as Plesseys and the General Register Office bringing hundreds of new families to the area. The feeling was far too many houses were going up but accompanied with too few facilities and the village was rapidly outgrowing itself. More major development was on the horizon however which would change the face of the parish and its community irrevocably.

MARCH 1924 - A TRAGIC CRASH

the usual cookery class of seven girls under their teacher Miss Booker
embled in the hut behind the Locks Heath Council School they were
sfully unaware of the trauma which awaited them. Cookery was a
w subject and each school in the area took a weekly lesson in the hut
ch had been built especially for the purpose.

-plane was circling the area piloted by a Mr. Montgomery, the son
Mrs. Montgomery of "Montgomery's Corner" where he was
ing with his fiancee, and it was seen to be in difficulty and making
ght for the hut. The general feeling subsequently was that the pilot
been showing off his manouvres and after a particularly
avagant dive had been unable to recover height.

girl in the hut remembers the teacher telling them not to gaze out
e window just as the aeroplane dived in their direction.

olane crashed into the hut at the point where the class was being
and an ll-year old girl Dora Ball was killed. Several girls were
ed, mainly by flying glass, and it was reported that Miss Booker the
her was badly disfigured. Dolly Mullins was the most badly injured,
ll her second teeth as a consequence and was very ill for some
afterwards as a result of the shock.

pilot escaped lightly with concussion and half the hut was
plished. Subsequently the hall was repaired and put to use as a
g-room for the school. The cookery lessons were transferred to the
orial Hall. Life in Locks Heath soon returned to normal and a quiet
e descended on the sleepy village. But for the parents of Dora Ball
s an incident which forced them to leave the district as they tried
rt a new life.

The Council School cookery class before...

MARCH 1924.

...the tragic crash

THE SECOND WORLD WAR IN LOCKS HEATH

The Warden Service in the area, manned by those worthy volunteers, started air raid precautions early in the year before the war. The sixty odd wardens, in conjunction with the First Aid and Rescue services, were credited with holding the first large co-ordinated exercise in the Fareham area in February 1939.

Many cheerful hours were spent in sand-bagging various posts and it came as an anti-climax for the volunteers when the early months of the war were marked by a complete absence of raids.

The Vicar, Rev. Keir Moilliet, leapt to the cause - "it appears to me that a parson who couldn't even help to fit a respirator or design a shelter-trench would be very little use to anybody in an emergency" - and he and some of his congregation Messrs. H. Manuel, R. Norris, Way, Perrett, Mrs. Luard and Captain Frearson were made Air Raid Wardens. Mr. Futcher took his training as an Auxiliary Fireman and his two sons as Dispatch Riders.

Soon after war was declared the local school was ordered to re-open with the proviso that "parents must use their own judgement as to whether they send their children to school or not". Before very long the school, like everyone else, had a shelter for the children to move to at the time of an air-raid.

A telephone post was established in the Head Warden's house and was staffed day and night for some months by a small band of devoted ladies. They were discouraged by the "phoney" war and subsequently continuous manning of the post was relaxed.

During the war years it is recorded that a dozen bombs altogether had fallen on Locks Heath directly. The ugliest incident of the war in the area occurred when an enemy bomber struck with two 50 kilo bombs, one of which scored a direct hit on a Sherman tank sited in Botley Road, Park Gate in preparation for D-Day. The tank loaded with ammunition blew up and five of their tanks were caught by the explosion. The continuous explosions went on for almost two hours and as a consequence two houses were totally demolished and many others were damaged. Large lumps of red hot metal from the tank fell over area up to several hundred yards away and live ammunition exploded and was blown over a wide area.

Unhappily two Canadian soldiers were badly burned when they jumped on to blazing vehicles and attempted to drive them clear. One of these soldiers later died in hospital and another civilian was seriously wounded. Two local wardens were to receive a Commendation of M from His Majesty the King for their work on that dreadful night.

Two slight civilian casualties were reported in Locks Heath during the War as a result of a blaze caused by exploding shells. The ARP Post's book showed 905 alerts recorded over the years but towards the end the war only night alerts were logged so the total certainly exceeded 1000. Plenty of false alarms and long weary alerts for the population and lots of unnecessary trips to the shelters.

It is reported that one of the first aerial battles of the Battle of Britain was fought partly over the area and provided stirring sights for reside often in brilliant sunshine. They could clearly see our Hurricane pilot diving on and attacking large formations of German aircraft.

Locks Heath residents had a grandstand view on many occasions of day-time dog-fights in the sky and would watch German bombers c ing the nearby airfield at Lee on Solent.

...ns sounded during an early summer evening then there would be ...t rush into the fields in the first instance to put out any bonfires ... had been lit earlier.

...e nights when Portsmouth and Southampton were blitzed in ...e fashion a few sticks were misplaced over Locks Heath but ...y fell wide of houses into open space. It is estimated that up to a ...ed bombs were distributed over the area, most of them falling ... the line of the railway and in the marsh land of the River Hamble.

...ents remember that some of the first to fall had screaming tubes ...dboard attached to their tail fins. One night brought two sticks of ... explosives which fell over Sarisbury Green and on through Locks ... One of these succeeded in demolishing the end of a house, ...ately without causing any casualties. The other fell in the low land ...en Lower Swanwick and Sarisbury Green. Only one house was ... set alight and was saved by valiant work through the night of the ...ens and neighbouring householders. The same night an oil bomb ...d a fire in a carriage drive in Brook Lane.

...esident even reported that a German flying boot had landed on ...of of his garden shed leaving the pilot to return with only a sock ...e foot.

...he momentous night two German aircraft strafed the area with ...vel machine gun fire. As they came in from the River Hamble the ...lanes fired incendiary bullets into the houses in Burridge Lane. ...there they swept back to the railway line, putting more bullets ...he Swanwick railway station, Nightingale Terrace and Barclays ... before finishing with a burst of fire into the British Legion where

two soldiers narrowly missed being hit.

Inevitably there was the odd unexploded bomb and the wardens were required to mark the spot with sticks in the ground and rapidly retreat. Later in the war the area had their first sight of the V1 flying bombs but the few that fell locally exploded harmlessly in the marsh land on the Sarisbury bank of the River Hamble. During the long period in which the South Wales district were bombed the German machines flew in from the Solent over Locks Heath and Park Gate. The Wardens grew used to them passing over and the Germans' timing was such that they knew when to expect the return trip.

As D-Day approached, during the latter years of the war, the area was flooded with troops and the side roads lined with tanks and guns. Residents found themselves having to dodge the hardware on a regular day-to-day basis and typically it was necessary to duck under the barrel of an anti-tank gun to enter a shop.

Most of the new residents were Canadian and many friendships were formed with great bonhomie. It was reported that a few days before D-Day a staff car drove down Bridge Road, which was lined with troops, carrying Lord Montgomery and Winston Churchill on their way to view the preparations.

The area had much to be proud of in their response to the War. Locally there were very efficient and active services in First Aid, Fire and Rescue, supplemented by the ever helpful Womens Voluntary Service. Up to twenty devoted women, under the leadership of Mrs. Idle, had formed the Locks Heath branch of the W.V.S. Besides organising an efficient rest centre, the ladies put themselves to work arranging the billeting of refugees from the Portsmouth and Southampton during the more severe air-raid periods. It is reported that a 'Pie Scheme' initiated by the

W.V.S. proved to be a real boon.

There was great emphasis on War Savings during those dark years and a W.V.S. Committee under the secretaryship of Mrs. Frierson made a good contribution from our area.

The Warden Service was highly thought of and the Head Warden was one of the three Bomb Reconnaissance Officers of the Fareham area who with his wardens had the distinction of staging a demonstration of the method of dealing with anti-personnel (butterfly) bombs, which was attended by leading representatives from the Army, Navy and County Police.

A Home Guard outfit - 14th Fareham Bn., Hants Home Guard, "K" Coy. (Locks Heath and Warsash) - operated in the area and prepared accordingly for their possible role.

At the height of the hostilities abroad a roll of names of those from the village serving in H. M. Forces was hung in the church. They were remembered at a special Communion Service held once a month, when relatives and friends were invited.

When peace came the parish looked for a way to create a worthy memorial to the Fallen. In the event it was decided that the memorial in St. John's Church should take three forms -firstly a tablet in oak, on the chancel wall, inscribed with the seventeen names of those of the parish who had laid down their lives; secondly the provision of an oak bar, hinged to the existing altar rail, to make the altar rail continuous; and thirdly the provision of a small steel safe in which the Blessed Sacrament could be reserved when there was any case of sickness in the parish. The plan was for sufficient of the Consecrated Elements to be placed in this safe immediately after the service of Holy Communion, prior to the Vicar's visit to the sick person. A War Memorial fund was launched to meet the cost of these items.

After the War the village erected a permanent memorial to the fallen the form of the Village Hall.

THE HELMET

The Wardens of the A.R.P.,
Feel cold, the same as you and me,
But when we toddle off to bed,
They may patrol the streets instead.
But when at night our Warden goes,
To quench the fires, lit by our foes,
With stir-up pump, he'll surely freeze,
On chilly evenings such as these.
And therefore, I, (of brain immense),
For one who works for our defence,
With knitting needles, wool and care,
Have made this cap for him to wear.

A poem by A.H.I.W
Xmas 1940

AR MEMORIALS

14-18

...emorial Screen in the South aisle of St. John's Church records 33 ...mes of those who fell in the 1914-18 War and was dedicated in a ...vice held on 11 June 1922. It reads:

...the glory of God and in proud and grateful memory of the men of ... parish who gave their lives in the great war.

...ed E. Beames   Percival D. Chapman
...ry C. Futcher   Walter Reed
...ry G. Smith   Alfred N. Harding
...erick Smith   Thomas Bolton
...ur Bridle   Charles E. Lush
...er C. Kent   George Beames
...ey H. Kite   Leslie C. Bowman
...les Matthews   George Williams
...d Bradley   Walter J. Smith
...k Frampton   Frank E. Goddard
...les G. Butcher   Thomas L. Reed
...K. Hutchinson   George R. Tanner
...d J. E. Pearce   Wilfrid H. Burt
...ur Bradley   Gordon C. Wellstead
...les J. Sansome   William E. Silsbury
...d Bailey   James W. Edmunds
...ur Price   Edgar Budd"

1939-45

As a commemoration of those of the parish who gave their lives in the Second World War the Parochial Church Council decided to install a memorial in the church. The memorial took the form of a gate to the Alter rail, a plaque inscribed with the 17 names of the fallen, and a small steel safe to hold the Sacred Elements when required for the Communion of the sick.

The plaque read as follows:

"In memory of those men of the parish who gave their lives in the war of 1939-45 the Altar Gate was placed in the church by grateful parishioners.

Christopher Carey   Maurice Chamberlain
Edward Gibbons   Austin Hanson
Charles Hill   William Jerred
Alan Knapp   Arthur Legg
Joseph Manuel   John Mansbridge
Peter Moor   Harry Osman
Ernest O'Donnell   Albert Smith
Owen Summers   Clive Waterman
Edwin Wearn"

An inventory of the memorials in St. John's Church has been recorded by the Royal British Legion and recorded in the Imperial War Museum.

THE FORMATION OF LOCKS HEATH WARD

It was not until 21 May 1950 that Locks Heath could claim its identity as a ward in its own right after previously being split between three adjoining wards for its entire existence.

The issue had been first raised by the two local churches in February 1944 when they presented a joint petition to Fareham Council containing over 1000 signatures, calling for adequate boundaries and representation for the area.

This was followed in June 1945 by a public meeting which heard from Mrs. Idle of the great difficulties experienced in public work by the lack of defined boundaries and from Mr. Richards of the inconvenience of a district containing up to 2000 people being without direct representation. After that meeting a committee under the initial chairmanship of Rev. Bernard Moilliet was formed to press the case and later a Locks Heath Electors' Association continued the pursuit of the aim through those five years.

Most of the credit for the new Ward goes to the personal campaign fought by the local County Councillor Walter Richards (known as 'Old Walt'). He was an outstanding personality in Locks Heath for many years and his record of service to the area, particularly on the County Council, was recognised in 1963 when a new road off Locks Road was named Richards Close by the Fareham Urban Council. This resolution was passed by the Council despite their avowed policy of not naming roads after councillors.

'Old Walt' was formerly Headmaster of Locks Heath Church of England School before his local government service and a resident of "Highlands" in Locks Road, the house which had figured so prominently in the early days of the village.

The new Ward was to be represented on the Council by three elected Councillors with an electorate of about 1350. It was to cover the area contained within the triangle bounded by Brook Lane, Hunts Pond Road and the Warsash-Titchfield Road together with Little Park and a small portion of Southampton Road.

The matter had been under consideration for five long years and by the persistent efforts of 'Old Walt' at Winchester and the backing of the Electors' Association the people of Locks Heath were now able to enjoy their right to local self-government and establish their own identity and boundaries. The interests of the village could now be adequately represented to the local Council.

ROMAN CATHOLIC CHURCH

For many years and until 1964 there was no Roman Catholic church serving the district and services were held in the Drill Hall at Park Gate.

The Roman Catholic Church of St.Margaret Mary was built in 1964 after the necessary funds had been raised by direct offerings and various fund-raising schemes. In a modern setting, reflecting post-war architecture, the church has seating for 230 and cost £30,000 in all. Several unique feature were incorporated, including cloisters and a prefabricated spire.

Within a few years an extension had been completed, in the form of brick-built Presbytery and Hall, and this has enabled the activities of ever-growing church to be widened.

FRENZIED DEVELOPMENT

January 1975 a structure plan was published which heralded an eruption of bricks and concrete which threatened to destroy the pleasant semi-rural character of Locks Heath in the next twenty years. The development plan for the Fareham Western Wards was to provide houses, flats, shops, offices and amenities for a population explosion of between 20,000 and 40,000.

The name of Locks Heath was threatened with extinction under the Boundary Commission changes and when 600 indignant residents signed a petition of protest they won the day - but only by one vote at the Council meeting.

The people of Locks Heath insisted on full participation in the discussions and the then Vicar, Bruce Carpenter, served on the executive of the "think-tank" Solent Plan Society set up by the locals to tell the planners what they wanted incorporated in what was almost a new town.

Bruce Carpenter was quoted at the time as saying - "We desperately need a town centre, community buildings, a library, more shops and all that to give the place a proper heart". We can now judge for ourselves how close Bruce's objectives have been met.

The 1980s Southern Hampshire had a buoyant economy with modern industrial estates dotting the countryside and the progress was reflected in the number of people attracted to the region. Homes had to be provided and urbanisation of Locks Heath encroached relentlessly.

Residents became used to being approached by developers' representatives wanting to buy up their properties or pieces of their gardens. Amazing sums were tendered and understandably many people succumbed to the realities of economic life and sold up.

A frenzy was in the air but residents accepted the large and small developments stoically, often despite being hemmed in on all sides by new houses or contractors' huts and equipment. Rows of newly-erected houses marched relentlessly across the Locks Heath landscape but there was concern that social facilities were being neglected in the rush to build.

The Locks Heath Centre today

INTO THE 70S WITH CHANGING COMMUNITY AND A NEW CENTRE

A local newspaper reporter visited Locks Heath in November 1974 and commented that the population struck him "as being in the predicament of the ancient city of Pompeii - existing beneath the crater of a smouldering volcano". Locks Heath folk knew what fate had in store for them - an eruption of bricks and concrete which would almost certainly destroy the pleasant semi-rural character of the village.

As the village waited for the publication of the structure plan the visitor was struck by the sheer anonymity of the place. Neatness and care was seen all around and little estates of houses were tucked away discreetly behind trees and hedges.

Development had stood still for several years in the area which had escaped the characterless sprawl of bricks which had despoiled nearby districts. A generation had grown up with a community spirit and a fierce sense of local patriotism.

'Communicare' had been evidence of the spirit of service in the community. Rev. Bruce Carpenter of St. John's had started a scheme in which a family in every road formed a link between the church and their neighbours, providing an information service and taking responsibility for elderly folk. This had expanded into 'Commmunicare', embracing all the area, with its own old people's mini-bus, luncheon club, and a team of voluntary co-ordinators who take turn to be on telephone duty for 24 hours. Doctors, clergy, health visitors, for example, could telephone the day's co-ordinator, who had a file index of people ready to answer every need and emergency.

The Community Centre was always heavily booked and that year of 1974 25 organisations had banded together to run a two-week festiv to mark the 80th anniversary of St. John's Church.

It was clear however that practically everybody wanted better ameniti on their doorstep but hardly anybody wanted to see the village atmosphere disappear.

Rev. Bruce Carpenter was certain - "We desperately need a town centre, with community buildings, a library, more shops, and all to gi the place a proper heart". He himself had served on the executive of the 'think-tank' Solent Plan Society, set up in order that local people could tell the planners in precise terms what they wanted incorporat in what would virtually be a new town.

On a more basic level the deplorable state of unmade roads in the village were the subject of bitter and prolonged complaint by resider Driving through some busy roads, such as Heath Road and Heath Rc North, involved nightmare rides over potholes, and through puddles and mud.

The village struggled for an identity and in that period of the early seventies one resident described it as a "no-man's-land village". He described how rates were paid to Fareham, water rates to Southampton, and how most of the shops were in Warsash or Park Gate. Mail for residents was often found to be addressed to Park G Titchfield Common or Sarisbury Green as evidence that people were shown to be confused by the boundaries.

The Hampshire topographical writer Ralph Dutton had summed it u rather succinctly by describing the area as a "rather lost piece of country". The late sixties had brought great changes to the village

ulation had risen from 1000 to 8000, the schools had expanded at
ntastic rate, and big employers like Plesseys and The General
ister Office had brought hundreds of new families to the area. In
context and in the light of future planned growth the framework
the long term planning intentions for the Action Area Plan were set
he South Hampshire Structure Plan which was approved in 1977 for
period up to 1991, later rolled forward to 1996.

planners reported that 'the most serious deficiency in the
ibution of shopping, community facilities and open space is in the
ral part of the plan area, at Locks Heath'. The considerable planning
lems needing to be remedied were reported to have been caused
he scattered pattern of settlement and inadequate provision of
e facilities, particularly (a) local shops in small groups, which did not
a range of services beyond day-to-day convenience goods
rements, (b) community facilities and (c) public open space, notably
ng fields, urban parks and children's play areas.

ng the objectives were the creation of a 'new identity for the area
whole by the development of a strong focus for the planned
munity of some 30,000 persons in the Western Wards', provision of
al, shopping and recreation facilities to serve new development
', provision of 'local employment opportunities in step with
ng growth' and the improvement of public transport facilities, and
and sewer infrastructure.

lan adopted in 1979 provided for housing development in three
es for an increase of about 4000 dwellings up to 1991, together
allocations of land for industry and offices at Segensworth and
Croft, for a new district centre, for distributor roads, and for
ls, churches, a police station and a fire station.

Progress in the housing areas was slow initially particularly with the
need to install a new sewerage system. By the end of 1986 the housing
development was on target and it emerged that more land was being
made available within the area than expected, as landowners brought
forward more of their plots for development. The original plan had
noted this possibility and the boundaries of individual areas had to be
varied when the aspirations of individual owners became known.

The planners noted that the densities in the residential areas were at the
upper end of the permitted ranges. It was clear that from the areas
developed and the in-filling permitted in built-up areas had yielded
more houses than forecast in the original plan.

It was estimated in 1987 that the potential number of new houses
could approach 5400 - that is, 1400 more than originally proposed. On
this basis it was felt that there was no need to allocate any further areas
of housing land to meet the area's needs to 1996.

For the proposed District Centre it was originally shown by the
developers Green Lane Developments that up to 50, 000 square feet of
retail floorspace and commercial facilities would be required but this
was shown to be inadequate and in 1982 permission was granted for
93, 000 square feet to be allocated. This was to be taken up with
46,000 square feet for a food store together with twenty shop units.

The beginning of the building work on the proposed District Centre was
marked by a Service of Dedication on the 44-acre construction site
attended by church representatives, civic leaders, building workers and
local people. Rev. Norman Chatfield conducted the open-air dedication
service which was attended by the vicars of Warsash and Sarisbury with
representatives of the Baptist and Roman Catholic churches in the area.

Finally Locks Heath Shopping Centre and Park, with an attractive clock tower at its head, was opened in time for Christmas trading in 1983 by the former boxer Henry Cooper in a suitable ceremony.

The provision of this centre, with community facilities, a library, woodland and a town park, are considered as helping to meet the objective to establish a strong community focus. The architecturally pleasing Centre is pleasing to the eye and is uniquely set with a backdrop of trees and open spaces. Car parking is free with more than 600 car spaces on one level and young children are catered for with a play area in the middle of the concourse.

In addition to the superstore and the 15 independent shops initially, the complex had its share of professionals and business people in offices dealing in such as holidays, fitness, mortgages, savings and house purchases. Other professional services were available on the first floor of the shopping centre.

The Traders Association has pursued a programme of events in the centre, including concerts, competitions and a Father Christmas at the appropriate time of the year.

A public house opened in the centre and the public were invited to suggest a name with a prize for the entry chosen. The name "Lock, Stock and Barrell" arose from the competition to name the establishment.

The national recession held back industrial development in the Wards but a 1985 survey showed that in the main employment area at Segensworth 40 firms were employing 1600 people.

At the time of writing the 'Southern Distributor Road', as part of the plan to connect the wards across from Fleet End to Abshot corner, is still under discussion and has faced mounting opposition from residents.

An ecumenical working party set up by the Portsmouth Diocesan Pastoral Committee gave advice to the planners up to 1979 on the predicted future requirements for religious accomodation. They concluded that a new Roman Catholic Church would be required and that St. Johns would seek to extend its hall and community rooms by further building and development, probably on the adjoining vicarage garden. Within a year or two however the diocese had reported that the Roman Catholic Church would no longer be required but that additional accomodation might still be necessary at St. Johns.

For a decade the area has been transformed as the builders and their bulldozers moved in to clear the ground of most of the open spaces that rows of newly-erected houses could march relentlessly across the landscape. The planners have wrung concessions from the developer that most of the estates have open spaces, greenways, and trees and shrubs in abundance to compensate.

It was the same ground which in most instances provided acre upon acre of productive strawberry fields and smallholdings which to past generations had been their livelihood. Then it was all countryside - mainly strawberry fields everywhere you looked. Then the community had a different focus and the area had a buoyant economy, as now, for a very different reason. That original focus had been the making Locks Heath and been responsible for its founding.

It's people who make places, not sticks and stones, and whatever the planners have perpetrated Locks Heath still retains its essential character, even if not a single strawberry patch remains.

"OWARDS THE YEAR 2000"

ook back at a Report from the Ecumenical Working rty, 6 April 1976

Working Party was formed in order to consider the future of the rches in the developing area of the Western Wards. Initially it was gested that there should be a new Roman Catholic Church in the t End area, that a large site should be secured near the new District tre for an Ecumenical Centre to serve as a new United Reformed rch and a Pastoral Centre for all churches in the area.

he event the Roman Catholic Church project was shelved but there continued discussion subseqently concerning proposals for church-ing in the light of a decision by the U.R.C to close their Locks Heath dings and concentrate work at nearby Sarisbury Green.

ussion proceeded about how the two churches might best work ther for shared buildings, worship, and ministry. A meeting held on uly 1976 agreed that the formation of an ecumenical "parish" ld be a natural development, with an equality of ministry and duct of joint services between the U.R.C. and St. Johns. The two sters, Norman Chatfield and Michael Playdon, circulated a paper iling the areas for discussion, following the meeting.

e end the Free Churches - U.R.C, Baptist and Methodist - financed gle Free Church appointment, which was mooted in the original ssions. The consequence was that St. Johns retained its own pendence and all Free Church members in the area were able to cipate in one church rather than commute to separate churches in areas for worship.

ST. JOHN'S CHURCH OF ENGLAND SCHOOL

It was in 1886 that a Tea and Concert Committee raised the £150 needed to build a Mission Church at the corner of Abshot Road and Hunts Pond Road. The first classes were held in the Mission Church the following year, both in the day and evening times.

When the Parish Church was built in 1894 the Mission Church became the village school, founded under the aegis of the Church of England.

LAND FOR THE VILLAGE SCHOOL
Conveyance dated 11 December 1894

"Montagu Henry Foster of Stubbington House, of 11 December 1894, conveyed to the trustees, Rev. Thomas Archer Meynell Archer Shepherd, William Green of Highlands, Louis Lynn of Brookheath, Frank Andrews of Upper Brook, and John Humley of Abshot Road, (one reverend, the rest gentlemen other than Humley a fruit-grower) assigned the plot of land on which the St. Johns Mission stood on the corner of Abshot Road and Hunts Pond Road to be used as a school for the education of children of the labouring, manufacturing and other poorer classes of the district, which said school shall always be in union with and conducted under the principles and in furtherance of the ends and designs of the National Society for promoting the education of the poor in the principles of the established church, the school to be under the management and control of a committee with the minister of Locks Heath Church at the head..."

During the later years of the last century most schools were established and subsequently maintained by the Church Authorities. Locally this involved the St. John's congregation in considerable expenditure for many years for the maintenance of the school and its playground. There were periods when a great deal of funding was required but the Church Council were determined not to let the school pass into the hands of the Education authorities.

John Pearce was the first Headmaster of the school from 1894 to 1915, being resident in the School-House with his wife. Shortly after his retirement he suffered a fatal heart-attack in Hunts Pond Road.

Pearce's successor Walt Richards was a major figure in the school's history, not only because of the length of his tenure from 1915 through to 1944, but by virtue of his influence and untiring efforts for the school, its pupils and parish affairs. On a personal note Walt was remembered by his former pupils for his distinctive plus-fours which he wore to school for over twenty years.

Walt Richards bought the "Highlands" on his retirement and became a successful strawberry-grower, like so many of his pupils. Walt played a prominent role in local government representing Locks Heath so effectively. After his death at the age of 90 in 1972 the Bookstall at the rear of St. John's Church was given in his memory.

Older Locks Heath residents who were former pupils recall the beadle, Mr Hicks, who would quickly pay a visit to your house on his tricycle if you failed to make an appearance at school.

It was during the 1930's that older pupils were transferred to Sarisbury Secondary School (now Brookfield Comprehensive School) and the school became a primary school rather than catering for all standards.

It fell to Miss Cummins to see the school through the effects of the 1944 Butler Education Act and in 1949 the Church Council agreed to change the school to a Controlled Status effective from February 195█

The tenure of Miss Cummins until 1966 saw a considerable amount c building and extension with the addition of modern facilities including magnificent hall and a playing field. Subsequently the original Missior Church, the oldest part of the building, has been converted into two classrooms.

The last Head of the Junior and Infants School was John Hansford wh when the school was re-organised in 1972, became Headmaster of t new Junior School off Admirals Road. He was succeeded by Mrs. Dor Rayner, Mrs. Hibberd and then Jean Corne.

The other long-established school in the parish is the County Primary Warsash Road, built in 1907. This was under the care of Headmaster Tom Richards originally, the brother of Walt, until 1914. In the 1970's new Infant School was built on the same site and when Park Gate Junior School opened at the same time to take the eight to eleven-ye olds of the area St. John's became an Infant School taking only five t seven-year olds.

Before that as a primary school it had taken five to eleven-year olds not without some difficulty. Up to 100 had been housed in the scho building but up to 60 more had to be taught in a part of the Free Church building in Hunts Pond Road.

In September 1995, under its Headteacher since January 1989 Jane Cambrook, the school reverts back to its role as a Primary taking fou eleven-year olds in addition to those accomodated at Park Gate.

e school is proud however to have retained its links with the Church
England , and its close relationship with St. John's Church,
oughout its own 100-year history and its various changes of status.

mer pupils' memories:

'e used to dry our coats around the stove"

ⅇ nurse used to come to school and look in our hair for nits"

ⅇ milk was left outdoors. It tasted sour in the summer"

sed to be ink monitor and fill up the ink wells"

ⅇ had to go to outside toilets, it was freezing in the winter"

ⅇ school dinners after the war were horrid. I hated tapioca (frog's
ⅅn)"

ⅰas often given two strokes of the cane for idling"

ESTERDAY'S CHILDREN"

and Toy Museum

Bernard Fuggle and Mrs. Sylvia Olin had been collecting dolls,
ⅇen's clothes and adult clothes for over twenty years when Mr.
ⅇⅇ first applied in 1983 for planning permission to turn part of his
ⅇ, "Locks Orchard" in Locks Road, into a museum. This was
ⅇted but a considerable delay ensued whilst the necessary finance
ⅇaised to convert the house and most importantly, at the insistence
ⅇ planning authorities, to lay a car-park.

The house had originally been built in 1894 as one of four identical
properties in Locks Heath. Known as "Briarleigh" the house fell into the
ownership in 1920 of Colonel Niven (the late film-star David Niven's
uncle) in the company of his invalid son. Villagers remember the pair
walking to church each Sunday in the company of Doctor Kingdon and
his family. Word has it that the young David Niven visited the house
during holidays from boarding school, before entering the acting and
film professions. Subsequently the house was in the ownership of
Admiral Scatchard and then, before the present occupancy, by a Mr.
and Mrs. J. Wilson who renamed it "Locks Orchard".

So it was that in October 1993, after first applying for the planning
permission ten years earlier, the museum, housed in the late Victorian
house, opened. Only about a third of the collection is on view at any
one time to allow for changes of display to be made. In addition only
about a half of the area of the museum is open to the public, until such
time as the rest of the area can be developed. Many of the dolls made
in the 1950's are collectors' pieces and the oldest exhibit of the nearly
3500 available for show is a 1835 doll.

The exhibition gives an insight into the social development and history
of the people involved in making them and it is fascinating to note how
the materials have changed over the years. At the time of writing the
venture needs to attract more support if it is to survive into the next
century and preserve the unique collection for another Locks Heath
generation.

THE LOCKS HEATH "GOOD COMPANIONS" CLUB (by Laurie Starks)

Some two dozen people were present at the inaugural meeting of the club which was held at the Memorial Hall on Monday 13 October 1958, with the Vicar Rev. Edwin Curtis in the chair.

It is recorded in the minutes that after prayers the Chairman welcomed Mr. L.C.C. Scaife, M.B.E. from the Winchester office of the Council of Social Service. Mr. Scaife confirmed that the club could be formed by a resolution and this was carried unanimously.

It was decided originally to meet on Mondays from 2 p.m. to 4 p.m. in the Memorial Hall and that the club be described as "A club of old people" under the name of the 'Locks Heath Good Companions Club'. A committee of 8 was then elected and since its formation the membership of the club has grown over the past 36 years to the present total of 85 members, aged from 60 plus to 95 years.

It was on 11 May 1992 that the club moved across the road to its present home in the new St. John's Church Hall.

The Committee work hard to create an interesting programme for the members week by week and in addition various outings are organised. Members visit ice-shows, theatres, the seaside and take trips into the countryside for tours which include the popular cream-teas. In addition the club organise a holiday for members each year.

The anniversary of the club's founding is marked each year with a cake and members regularly organise bring and buy sales, a bazaar and bingo sessions.

The Good Companions work for charity by having a weekly collection through their 'charity box' and by book sales. Their efforts over the years have led to donations being made to many local and national charities.

LOCKS HEATH WOMEN'S INSTITUTE

(by Joan Renton)

During the summer of 1933 several ladies in the village met to discuss forming a Locks Heath Women's Institute. The movement had been brought over from Canada where it strived to educate rural women about home hygiene and improve their culinary and household skills.

The 19 October 1933 saw the first meeting in the Memorial Hall, where it still meets today. The main purpose then was to improve and develop the conditions of rural life and the W. I. motto was 'For Home and Country'. Their magazine still carries that title.

Sadly the early records are lost but the 1935 Programme shows the President, Mrs. Blake of Little Wood, Sarisbury with a Committee consisting of affluent village ladies. One of the talks was 'Links with Empire', with a competition, a Knitted Bathing Suit and the entertainment was Recitations. Plenty of fun and games then!

As the village grew in the 1980's, the W.I. expanded to 100 members in October 1985 the Lockswood W.I. was formed as a morning meeting.

Today the W.I. learn computer programming and car maintenance, take courses at their own college, have parties, choirs, drama, dance, create crafts and yes, still make jam. But most of all they value the fellowship of the W.I. and its place in the community.

OCKS HEATH DAY CENTRE

Locks Heath Day Care Centre Group first came together as an
ormal association in May 1984. The group members were together
olved to provide Day Care for the frail and elderly in the local
mmunity. The group was made up of representatives from local
mmunity organisations such as Communicare, Swanwick Lions and
Rotary Club, together with the local churches and some professional
erts.

y were conscious of the fact that the growing community in the
contained many elderly people for whom no essential services were
g provided.

r assuming charity status in December 1985 the group issued an
on Statement which took account of a factual study of local needs
careful research. The study stated that 90 persons could benefit
the provision of a local day centre, which compared with the 21
ons who were able to find a place at the Kershaw Day Centre in
ham. The study revealed that there was a waiting list of the
tern Wards elderly ready to use that Kershaw Centre.

Group gained recognition from the local Council and the Health
ority and was made up of three representatives of each of the local
nisations and churches together with representatives of the
tory bodies and local G.P's. John Bullen, who had been the original
r of the parish magazine, was the representative nominated from
hn's Church and he went on to give distinguished service in the
e of the Centre.

Action Statement was adamant that a 30-place Day Centre was
ssary and should ideally be located at the Lockswood Centre on

that part of the land which had been reserved by the Council for
Community Health use. They concluded that a Centre of that size
would be fully utilised by 1995 on present population growth
predictions and at the time of the publication in 1986 the building cost
was estimated £186, 000 with £26, 000 per annum required for
running costs.

The Group had the task of finding the means to finance the
undertaking. It was clear that part of the funding would be provided by
the health services but that a substantial proportion would have to be
found through charity support and public appeal.

In the first instance the Group were anxious to provide immediate day
care for the elderly on that waiting list. They negotiated with the
Management of Coldeast Hospital for the temporary use of
accommodation there.

As a consequence a service catering for up to 12 persons each day for 3
days per week was opened in the Assembly Rooms of the hospital in
September 1988. The Group set themselves the task of raising £9000
for necessary building adaptations and equipment. Up to 50 volunteers
to form carer teams on a rota basis had to be recruited, together with
volunteer drivers. By this time a Supporters Club had been formed.

The Group knew that the Service would have to operate at the Coldeast
Hospital for at least five years whilst a larger centre was funded and
built at Lockswood Centre on the site which by now had been reserved
by the Fareham Borough Council.

The Service at Coldeast was run by three teams of helpers over the
three days. Their aim was to provide a regular day out for the frail and
elderly who might live alone or be house-bound, and also to provide

some relief for those carers looking after an elderly member of the family at home. They offered the opportunity to socialise and make new friends, have a hot lunch, enjoy entertainment and for the disabled it was possible to have a bath by the use of the specially adapted and equipped bathroom.

The fund-raising continued apace and their efforts were rewarded when, in recognition of the amount of £50, 000 raised by the community, the Portsmouth and South-East Hants Health Commission announced in the spring of 1995 that they had approved a grant of £300, 000 towards the building costs. This prompted the Group to announce that the building work for the Lockswood Day Centre would commence in August 1995 and would open in the early Spring of 1996 under the control of a Management Committee. The funding by the Commission enabled the fund-raising to concentrate on the furnishing and equipping of the new Centre.

The Centre was to be furnished by asking local bodies like schools, churches and clubs to take over a room. The idea was for such bodies to be associated with these rooms on a permanent basis and they would raise the money to furnish their rooms by organising events. In the first instance it was announced that Brookfield School would fund a hobbies room in conjunction with other schools in the district.

The Day Centre would provide Care services on five week days for up to 150 frail or handicapped older people living in the area with chiropody, hairdressing, assisted laundry and assisted bathing facilities available. Recreation, entertainment and meal facilities and the other facilities would be under the control of a paid supervisor who would be supported by a large team of volunteers. The service would include the provision of a hot meal and transport to and from the centre where necessary.

In addition the Centre would be aiming to provide advice and counselling services both for the benefit of the clients and their carers and also provide visits and outdoor activities on an occasional basis.

The Group had to recruit and train extra volunteers so that the larger team could be formed in support of the small team of professionally qualified and experienced staff.

At other times the Centre could be used by other community groups, clinics and classes and it was even envisaged that accommodation for other services such as the Citizen Advice Bureau and the Red Cross could be provided.

As this book is printed volunteers were being recruited whilst the build of the centre commenced. Everyone involved was sharing the exciteme of being one of the pioneers in this ambitious community project.

LOCKS HEATH AND DISTRICT ABBEYFIEL SOCIETY

This branch was formed in November 1971, with the Bishop of Portsmouth, Dr.John Phillips, as their president, and support was forthcoming immediately from the League of Friends, through their chairman Jimmy Will, Locks Heath Rotary Club, the Good Companic the Women's Institute, and the Sarisbury School Community Service

Initially the Society were looking for a large house or a piece of land which to build a house to accommodate up to nine elderly lonely fo from the area.

Support was anticipated from the Fareham Urban District Council so

t many elderly people who moved into such accommodation would
ve their own houses which could be occupied by younger families.

alification for residents was loneliness and ability to pay a modest
ekly amount for their rooms and keep. Residents could take some of
r own furniture to their room. A warden and housekeeper would
pare meals and serve them in a communal dining room and there
uld be a large sitting room as a general lounge.

d raising was put in hand and at a review meeting in September
2 it was announced that £1000 had been received from numerous
l groups.

ntually thanks partially to a government grant the Society was
oled to purchase Locks Farm and The Stables in Hunts Pond Road
convert these properties accordingly.

sequently the Society was bequeathed a further property,
ryside" at Hamble and are accordingly looking at means to fund
necessary conversion.

PULATION FIGURES

the Census figures the growth of Locks Heath as a result of the
ern Wards development can be gauged.

-	5900
-	6300
-	13800
cted 1998 -	14900

THE NEW LOCKS HEATH FREE CHURCH

After renting the old Congregational Church sited about 100 yards
south of Dimmock's Corner the Locks Heath Free Church had seen their
congregation grow from a handful to 175 in nine years. It was therefore
decided to build a new church to the south of the old church on the
east side of Hunts Pond Road between the junctions with Prelate Way
and Netley Road.

Under their minister Rev. David Clarkson the new church held its first
service on 14 January 1990 and the Sanctuary seated 250 people. An
overflow for a further 150 was sited in a small hall at the rear.

The hall could be used for fellowship and meetings and there was also a
sports hall large enough for badminton, a fully fitted kitchen, a bookstall,
a creche, a Baptistry and a number of small rooms and vestries. Further
rooms for meetings, study and clubs can be found upstairs.

The overall cost was £540,000 and this was raised by the local
membership and through grants from Baptist organisations.

At the opening, with Rev. David Clarkson (right)

A CENTURY OF Worship

PART ONE - THE FIRST 50 YEARS

Century of Worship
IE ST JOHN'S CHURCH STORY
rt One

A Place to Worship

is Lynn , born in 1850 and originating from a peasant family in
ey where his father was a shepherd, had not only put Locks Heath
he map by realising its unique strawberry-growing potential but was
to be the prime mover behind establishing a place to worship in
area.

re moving from Curdridge Lynn was friendly with the large
lectual Lukin family and in 1882 when some of the Lukins moved to
s Heath, occupying the Highlands Farm Estate, Lynn moved in with

e was no place to worship and Lynn organised religious meetings at
dmill Farm in Hunts Pond Road. At Hook Church at Warsash there
overcrowding and it was felt imperative to build a chapel at
field Common to seat 150 at a proposed cost of £350. Despite
thirds of the money being promised, an appeal to the Church
missioners, endorsed by the Bishop of Winchester, was refused.
and the Lukins swung into action and secured loans from local
owners and tradesmen. Lynn formed a 'Tea and Concert
mittee'and raised £150 for the construction of a Mission Church at
orner of Abshot Road, on land given by Montagu Foster of
ington. The foundation stone was laid in a snow storm in
mber 1886 on St. John's Day and the Choir had walked from Hook

in the adverse weather.

The following year an Anniversary Tea and Concert was held at the Jam
Factory (lent by Lynn, Hoar & Co.) near the "Sir Joseph Paxton" and the
crowds were such that two sittings were necessary for the food. It is
reported that 'many had to wait some time before being served'. Lynn
spoke of the 'moral improvement of the Common' since the opening of
the Mission and appealed for subscriptions. He asked the men 'to give
up a little beer and tobacco and the women to do without a feather or
some trifling thing and give the savings to the house of God'.

Mary Lukin gave £50 but Lynn was the most generous and became the
Mission Warden, as well as taking charge of the Children's Services. It
was said that the worshippers of St. Mary's Hook had been so moved by
their efforts that they were happy to "adopt" the new church as their
"Son", John being a member of the family of Mary as Elizabeth's child.
The building was completed within a year and the Vicar at Hook-with-
Warsash , Reverend Henry Wilkinson Bull, would regularly officiate at
services at the Mission Church at 9 a.m. and 7 p.m. to fit in with his
own parish's commitments. His curate Rev. G. Pratt looked after the
Mission temporarily and Rev. C.L. Perry and Rev. R. Burton would also
visit to preach on a regular basis. Early in 1891 Rev. Mills Robbins, who
lived in Abshot Road. took charge of the Mission Church. Robins also
rented a property on his own initiative at Fleet End for religious
meetings but when he moved on at the time of the division of the
parish this mission came to an end.

Mills Robbins was reputed to have been a man of great personality
starting evening classes for men, organising a cricket team and
introducing rugby to the area. It appears that this latter move was not a
success and association football had to be substituted. By June 1893
with the arrival of their own Vicar Rev. T. Archer Shepherd the Mission

Church at Locks Heath provided three services on a Sunday with one on Wednesday, together with day and night schools, for almost eight years.

2. A New School with a New Church

By now the ever-growing population of Locks Heath, shown to be 740 in 1899, warranted a junior school and the Mission Church was converted to a Church of England School in 1894 with a small payment expected for attendance. The early records show an average attendance at the Mixed Day School of 106, from age 5 until leaving school at 14. . The conversion was to coincide with the start of the erection of our St. John's Parish Church.

The growth of worship in the area was marked by the forming of the ecclesiastical parish of Locks Heath out of the parishes of Hook, Sarisbury and Titchfield in February 1893.

In 1894 a piece of land at the corner of First Park and Church Road was donated by Mr. Montagu Foster, who had a Naval Preparatory School at Stubbington, specifically as the site for the building of St. John's Church.

The foundation stone was laid by Augusta Bradshaw from Abshot House, the grand-daughter of Mr. Arthur Hornby, in recognition of the family's endowment to St. Johns. The inscribed stone can be seen set into the north-east corner of the church still. It is said that a two-pound kilner jar, containing artefacts of the day (as a "time-capsule"), was buried under the foundation stone. Mr. Hornby had given the land for the nearby St. Mary's, Hook church and endowed it similarly. The Hornby family had held manorial rights over a large part of the Common before its enclosure.

When the building was completed in 1895 it was reported to be of Swanage stone with Bath stone dressings. The church was from desig by the late Mr. Ewan Christian, an architect from London, and consist of chancel, nave, south aisle, organ chamber and vestry north porch with an eastern turret containing a bell.

The church and parsonage had been built and the living endowed ou of funds left for the purpose by the late Mrs. Charlotte Hornby. She h died five years earlier in 1890 and her prominent grave, with that of husband, can be found in the St. Peter's Titchfield church-yard. The living was expressed to be for perpetual curacy with a gross yearly va of £150. There were immediate plans for the Mission Room to be use as a school.

LOCKS HEATH DISTRICT (Now New Parish)

A copy of the instrument:

"We the Ecclesiastical Commissioners for England, acting in pursuance of the 'New Parishes Acts, 1843 and 1856' hereby approve the Church or Chapel which has been erected within and for the District of Locks Heath which District is situate in the County of Southampton and in the Diocese of Winchester and was constituted under the Authority of the said Acts.

In Witness whereof we have hereunto set our Common Seal this thirty firs day of October in the year One thousand eight hundred and ninety five.

Sealed by the Ecclesiastical Commissioners for England in the presence of Francis Cobb, Registrar, Ecclesiastical Commission, 10 Whitehall Place, Westminster."

Early Days under the First Incumbent

church was duly consecrated and the first incumbent was the
erend T.A.M. Archer-Shepherd, M.A., who held the post for the next
years until 1908. In common with most parishes the church was
ported financially almost entirely by the three or four rich families in
vicinity. The Bradshaws at Abshot, the Fieldings at West Hill and the
nbys at Hook had their names at the top of the subscription lists
en any appeals for funds were made. Their involvement did not stop
e - Lady Louisa Fielding ran a Mother's Meeting on Wednesdays
ughout the winter and Mr. T.B. Bradshaw was captain of both the
nfield Common cricket and football teams when they were formed.

he time of the consecration the area of the parish was recorded as
1 acres and the population as 740 but said to be "increasing
dly". By 1899 the parish records show that 6 males were confirmed
year, with 17 baptisms and the number of communicants on the
toral roll shown to be 47. The Day School Register showed 146
dren on the books, but with an average daily attendance of 106.
Sunday School had 128 on its books in 1899 with an average
day attendance of 81 being infants under 7, boys and girls under
care of 9 teachers, 4 male and 5 female. .

contributed further to the growth of religion in the area by selling
t in Hunts Pond Road to a Mr. Hicks for the building of the
gregational Chapel built in 1902 - subsequently United Reformed
then the Free Church until its recent demolition.

r than Lynn early stalwarts at St. Johns were W.J. Oliver, J. Selway,
reen, and T.W. Roome who took up posts as churchwardens in
e early years.

4. A Tragic End and a New Beginning

After the collapse and tragic death of Rev. Archer-Shepherd whilst
robing in the vestry before the evening service on Sunday May 17th
1908 the parish came under the care of the Rev. Brent R. Neville, an
Irishman from the Isle of Wight, with the assistance of a Curate Rev.
Antony M. Topp. The coming years were marked by large congregations
with the Harvest Thanksgiving Services in particular, reflecting the
agricultural nature of the area, attracting numbers approaching 500
each year, but with only a very small proportion as communicants.

April 1909 saw the first-ever Confirmation Service at St. John's and that
and the Memorial Service on the death of King Edward V11the
following year brought huge congregations which were all the more
remarkable given the size of the parish of less than a thousand.

By the autumn of 1913 the Rev. Brent Neville's health was such that he
would clearly be at risk by spending another winter in this country or
indeed the cold church building. He accepted a chaplaincy abroad but
in any event was advised to retire on his return.

5. The First P.C.C., Hard Times and the Arrival of John Robinson

The arrival of a new Vicar in the form of the Rev. John Robinson
coincided with the formation of a Church Council and the very first
committee was charged with setting up a Poor Fund,

As the Great War came to an end in 1918 a scheme to build a Parish
Room, subsequently to be proposed as a Memorial Hall, was embarked
upon and, largely thanks to the unstinting efforts of the congregation,

the necessary funds were raised to enable the Hall to be built and opened in 1922. The same year also saw the dedication of the Memorial Screen which had been erected in church with the names of the fallen inscribed thereon.

Times were hard and the church suffered such that the state of the finances made it impossible for the quota to be paid over to the diocese, for the first time, The labour problems and in particular the coal-strike were felt in Locks Heath. The winter of 1926 brought a freezing church for worshippers as coke and anthracite could not be obtained to feed the fires.

The sudden death of the much-loved Mrs. N.A. Robinson, the Vicar's wife, in 1928 cast a shadow over the parish and hastened the retirement of her husband two years later.

6. Another World War Around the Corner

Shortly after the arrival of his successor Rev. Keir Moilliet the vicarage was provided with a water supply and then a few months afterwards with electric light.

The School in the village was an important part of church life and required considerable resourcing in the way of funding and management. A considerable amount from church funds had to be expended on a regular basis to maintain such items as the roof and playground but in 1937 the Church Council resisted the chance to dispose of their control to the Education Authority.

As war clouds gathered St. Johns became involved in 1938 in its first major involvement with an overseas parish when out of the blue it was approached by its namesake church located in a small town called Ri[...] in a remote part of Alberta in Canada. They appealed for funds to provide a resident minister and from then on for many years the proceeds of the collection from the Patronal Festival Sunday passed t[...] the little congregation on the other side of the world.

7. Playing a Full Part in the War Effort

During the Second World War the Vicar and his congregation played their full part in the war effort as wardens, dispatch riders, home gu[...] or voluntary workers.

One particular effort did end in complete frustration however. When the Ministry of Food called for supplies of jam Locks Heath was an obvious centre with its readymade supply of fruit. The Rev. Moilliet rallied his congregation and a ton was quickly made and stored read[...] for collection. The frustration came when the Ministry failed to colle[...] despite continued reminders and the jam was left to go bad.

Much of the organisation of the civilian war effort was focused on t[...] neighbouring districts of Warsash, Sarisbury and Titchfield and this [...] the residents of Locks Heath again bemoaning their lack of identity. local churches were instrumental in 1944 in obtaining and submittir[...] petition to the Fareham Urban District Council to make Locks Heath into a separate ward. which was initially unsuccessful, but later successful…

Continued in Part Two. See Page 79.

EV. THOMAS ARCHER MEYNELL ARCHER
EPHERD, B.A.

. Johns 1893-1908)

Archer Shepherd was born in Dublin in March 1856, the son of the
John Shepherd, Vicar of Treniglos in Cornwall. He gained a B.A
ee at Oxford and was admitted to Corpus Christi College in
bridge in 1878.

as ordained in Bristol in 1882 and was a curate in Tewkesbury,
ourne, Normanton and locally at Bishops Waltham before moving
ke charge of St. Johns Mission at Locks Heath in 1893. He took
Lynn as his first church warden.

Archer Shepherd changed his name legally in 1898 to add a
en to become Archer-Shepherd for no apparent reason. Ten years
on 17 May 1908 he collapsed and died in the vestry at St. Johns
t robing in preparation for the evening service.

nder two years earlier on 18 April 1906 at the age of fifty he had
ed Caroline Harriet Gunner, the youngest daughter of Charles
er.

CHURCH WARDENS' ACCOUNTS FROM EASTER 1905 TO EASTER 1906

RECEIPTS

Bal. in hand from 1904	£1.17.7½..
Offertories for:	
Gen.Church Expenses	£30.10.2.
Parish Charities	£5.19.0.
Sick and Needy Fund	£2.12.4.
South Hospitals	£2.8.9.
Soc.for Prom.Gospel	£1.14.3.
Winchester Diocese	£1.4.0.
Curate's Soc.	£1.4.0.
Choir Lads	£1.0.6.
London Charity Hosp.	6.0.
National Society	13.6.
Donation - Engraving stone	12.6.
Deficit -1906	£2.18.6.
	£53.1.1½.

Signed:
Walter J.Oliver, John Selway
Churchwardens

PAYMENTS

Bal. paid to Choir Lads	£1.17.7½.
Organist's Salary	£10.10.0.
Caretaker's Salary	£8.0.0.
Anthracite Coal	£3.18.0.
Oil	£2.4.7.
Organ tuning/repairs	17.6.
Washing surplices	£1.18.0.
Communion wine (5 botts)	17.6.
Wood/cleaning materials	6.6.
Printing	3.7.
Church garden work	6.0.
Cab hire for Bishop	4.0.
Engraving	£1.7.6.
Fire insurance prem.	£3.18.0.
National Society	13.6.
South Hospital	£2.8.9.
S.P.G.	£1.14.3.
Winchester Dioc.	£1.4.0.
Sick & Needy Fund	£2.12.4.
Choir Lads	£1.0.6.
London Charity Hosp.	6.0.
Parish Charities	£5.19.0.
Curates' Soc.	£1.4.0.
	£53.1.1½.

Rev. Brent Neville with his congregation in their "Sunday best" (c. 1910)

Billy Lambden holds the standard as the choir parades, with Dr. Oliver (left),
Rev. John Robinson (centre) and Mr T. Yaldron (right) in the middle row (c. 1920)

WILLIAM (BILLY) LAMBDEN

e of St. Johns' greatest servants

he hundred years of its existence St. John's Church has seen many
oted and long-serving members but few can compete with the
orts of William Lambden.

as in 1903 that he was appointed at a vestry meeting as the verger
full-time capacity. Subsequently he was also to fill the positions of
on and clerk with his pay at a sparse level. The words 'faithful, loyal
willing' do little justice to his service to the church and successive
mbents.

n his wife and daughter Doll in a small cottage, "Holmleigh" in
ts Pond Road, opposite the school, he was also a grower but spent
y spare minute in the church at every job which required doing. He
ld even play his part in services by putting his singing voice to good
by leading the chanting of the psalms with the Vicar each Sunday.
y single service in church for over forty years found him present and
ect for his various duties, including the ringing of the bell as
ired.

A NIL RETURN

The St. John's Parish Registers show only one occasion in the one
hundred year history when it was recorded that 'none were present' so
that the service was cancelled. The date of this sole occurrence was
Sunday 16 September 1917 and the service concerned was the 8 a.m.
Holy Communion.

CARRIED ALL THE WAY

When Mr. J .Selway, a churchwarden at St. John's in the early days of
the century, died his coffin could not be carried by a hearse to his burial
at Sarisbury. In accordance with his wishes his coffin had to be walked
from Locks Heath with the aid of relays of bearers. Their task was made
no easier by the snow laid heavily on the ground at the time of his
burial in midwinter.

THE TITCHFIELD STONE

Titchfield, through its ancient 'minster' church, was clearly the "mother
parish" to Locks Heath. In recognition of this St. John's P.C.C. decided in
August 1938, at the instigation of the Vicar, Rev. Bernard Moilliet, to
insert a piece of carved work of Norman origin, obtained from St.
Peter's Church at Titchfield, in the wall of their church.

It was part of the capital of a pillar dating back to about 1100 A.D. The
opportunity to insert this ancient piece of church history arose when the
masons were working at St. John's repairing a 'corbel' which had fallen
a year previously.

REV. BRENT RICHARD ROBERT NEVILLE, M.A. (St. Johns 1908-15)

Rev. Brent Neville succeeded Rev. Archer-Shepherd after the latter's sudden death and coincidentally like his predecessor had also been born in Dublin. He obtained his degree at Trinity College in Dublin and was subsequently ordained by the Bishop of Limerick in 1886.

Brent Neville was first a curate at Trealee in Ireland before becoming to this country and taking up his first incumbency as Rector at Greenstead in Essex in 1893. Appointments at Abbotsbury in Dorset (1897-1902) and St. Lawrence on the Isle of Wight (1902-07) followed before his arrival in Locks Heath in 1908.

Brent Neville enjoyed a seven-year popular stay at St. Johns and was known for the regularity of his visits to parishioners with his pony and trap. Then during the First World War he moved to France to become Chaplain of Holy Trinity at Pau.

At the end of the war Rev. Brent Neville returned to this country and for his final post took up the vacant Rector's post at Holbrook in Suffolk. He retired in 1933 and stayed in the area at Felixstowe before his death in 1940.

GNES'S STORY

(▼ Agnes Reading)

as born in 1910, brought up in Locks Road and went to school at
t End School. I lost my father at age 11 and left school at 14 to go
service at St. Johns Vicarage for Rev. John Robinson. I worked there
l my marriage and lived in with the cook.

ore that my mother had been the Sunday School Superintendent
I had been used to being taken to the Vicarage in my pram whilst
gave her instruction to the children.

Vicar then was Rev. Brent Neville and his wife had a lady
panion who looked after me during the services and became my
mother.

ather was a market gardener - the men were either growers or
rs - and from an early age I was used to being up early at 5 a.m.
ng the season so that my mother and sisters could go into the fields
ck. Even the Vicar got the bug, growing strawberries on land at the
om of the Vicarage garden.

child I was forbidden to go out in the fields in case I trod on the
es. Even before I was five however I was found a job, sitting on a
for hours under the cherry trees and having to rattle stones in a tin
ghten the birds away.

ember the the suppliers calling round before each season and
tiating prices with my father. I recall the trips two or three times
ay on the cart to the railway station and the hours of queueing
that entailed.

How fascinated I was by the packing and loading on to the trains
involving the squads of small boys. They had to be small enough to
squeeze and crawl between the shelves to get the baskets packed into
every spare space in the carriages.

We lived in "Lock's Cottage" in Locks Road but later moved to
"Sunnyside" in Church Road.

Rev. John Robinson was a well-known figure moving around the parish
on his bicycle but it was a small congregation in those days. The only
time I can remember the church being packed was on Armistice Sunday
when the veterans paraded and marched to the accompaniment of the
Locks Heath Band.

Mr. Lambden was the verger and with his wife and daughter worked
long and hard for many years for the church. I remember them coming
to the Vicarage every Saturday for water with which to clean the
church.

It was the verger's job to ring the bell on a death in the parish being
notified. The custom was to ring it three times on a male death, twice
for a lady and one for a child. After a pause he would then ring out the
whole age of the deceased. When that was all over Mr. Lambden would
then come over to the Vicarage and tell us who had died and so we
servants were often the first to know.

Rev. John Robinson with his congregation (c. 1920)

A charabanc outing to the seaside, from St. Johns

REV. JOHN C. ROBINSON, M.A.

(St. Johns 1915-30)

Rev. John Robinson was educated and prepared for the ministry at Hatfield Hall, Durham, was ordained as a priest in 1891 and served h first curacy in Coventry.

John Robinson moved to the South in 1902 to Bournemouth at St. James Church as a curate before taking charge of All Saints at West Southbourne. He was there for thirteen years and then came to Lock Heath in 1915 during the First World War.

The private means of Rev. John Robinson enabled him to be generou and giving to village causes and employ two maids and a gardener, v whom and his wife shared meals nevertheless. The Robinsons were childless but Mrs. Robinson took charge of the Sunday School which thrived at the Abshot Road Day School.

During that First World War John Robinson helped form the Locks Heath Company of Volunteers and took his turn on night duty at Fareham Railway Station to guard high explosives being held there t await delivery to Gosport.

Rev. John Robinson also lost his wife during his incumbency at Lock Heath and her untimely sudden death at the age of 52, during her night in a nursing home after suffering from phlebitis, affected him greatly.

John Robinson was remembered as a quiet gentle priest by the sma congregations of the day and he would not have claimed to have b a great orator. He enjoyed the company of the children of the villag would often play the piano and lead the singing at their parties.

Robinson was a well-known figure with his pipe ever-present and was regularly seen out on his bicycle around the village. He took a ding role in the move to build the Memorial Hall, and was the mbent at St. Johns for fifteen years until 1930 before retiring to live etersfield, where he had bought some land.

his retirement he married Miss Rachel Oliver, the daughter of Dr. J. the Vicar's churchwarden for some years. During his incumbency Oliver had played a leading role in the Girls Friendly Society.

ter moved to Lymington but died at age 94, on the anniversary of rst marriage.

ARMISTICE - A THANKSGIVING

on 11 November 1918 at 11 a.m. that it was announced that the stice had been signed to signal the end of the Great War.

everywhere else the flags came out in Locks Heath and by midday al members of the congregation had congregated at Church er. It is recorded that an impromptu ten-minute service was held , as a thanksgiving.

evening we are told that the usual daily service of Intercessions at . was attended by a flood of worshippers such that "they owed the War Corner into all the adjoining seats".

Wednesday evening a large congregation took part in a ksgiving Service. We are told that "with coal so scarce it was priate to have no fire but with such a packed church it was

unnecessary". Rev. John Robinson recorded that "As if nature would conspire to remind us of the need of economy in light, towards the close of the service a dark November sky made hymn books useless. Still, they could be dispensed with, as we sang with thankful hearts the hymns that have cheered and helped us during the four years of war".

LOCKS HEATH CHURCH FAIR/FETE

From very early in the life of our church it has been the custom to hold an annual fair (or fete as it has been called since the fifties) in the village, not only as a vehicle for fund raising, but mainly for the community and fellowship benefits.

Always a summer event, for the first quarter of this century the fair was traditionally held on a Wednesday, usually after the early August Bank Holiday weekend. Invariably it was held in the grounds of one of the large houses in the area, by kind permission of the owner. In recent years the Vicarage garden was a popular venue but now that the vast open spaces available to the parish are gone it is restricted to the grounds of the church and the car-park. In those early years it was organised by two separate committees, one composed of men and the other of women.

For many years the fete expenses were met through the generosity of Mrs. Roxburgh. In 1924 the entrance fee was one shilling up to 5 p.m. and then sixpence as the proceedings continued into the evening. A Dance in the cool air of the early evening was a regular occurrence but there was "a small charge for dancing on the Vicar's lawn".

Very often musical entertainment during the afternoon was provided by such as the Locks Heath Band, the Hook Boys Band, or the

Southampton Temperance Band hired for a small fee. A regular feature for many years were the 'Bartletts Amusements' with their roundabouts and fairground attractions, hired for £5.

The fair was not the same without the children's fancy dress carnival, the baby show or pram parade, and displays such as square- or country-dancing. A great fund-raiser was always the raffle and for many years the one prize traditionally on offer was a bicycle purchased by the committee.

In May 1931 however the raffle was discontinued at the request of Rev. Keir Moillet as he was "against the principle of betting and sweepstakes generally". Its interesting to note that by 1947, and after his departure , not only had the raffle been reinstated but on odd occasions a fortune teller was one of the main attractions.

Light Refreshments of various forms have always been available but in the early part of the century a big appetite was required when 'pig-roasting' was on the menu. For some early post-war years the fete had a theme such as the 'Romany Life' when gipsies with their caravans and wares were invited. Another theme was the 'Wild West' and the big attractions were a guest appearance by Big Chief Sitting Bull and an entry into the Mysterious Wigwam.

For the first fifty years or so the proceeds from the day's events had to be put to parochial uses. For many years the proceeds had to be devoted to the repayment of the Hall debt, maintenance of the Hall itself and items such as a stove and a piano which could not be funded from the lettings fees. When the Hall debt was repaid, the fete proceeds passed to such funds as Diocesan Quota, Heating, Lighting, Church repairs, and a significant amount over the years went for School maintenance.

For many years however up to the present time the entire proceeds have been given to charities. In recent times an additional summer attraction has been the annual Locks Heath Carnival organised by the Swanwick Lions Club for the benefit of the local charities which they support and held in the recreation ground in Hunts Pond Road.

A 'World Fair' was held in June 1969 to mark the end of the week-lor 75th Anniversary Celebrations in aid of missionary work. More than 1100 people heard a pilot with the Missionary Aviation Fellowship op the fair and describe how the funds would be used to enable him to reach primitive tribes in Africa. Stallholders were dressed in the costur of many lands. In the event £20 was raised for the missionary work.

In 1974 the church fete was cancelled for one year and made way fc the fete which was the centrepiece of the two week-long 80th anniversary festival in the village. The fete that year was opened by L Montagu of Beaulieu and was held at Brookfield School being a combined church and school venture. An 1890's style cricket match, a knockout' tournament, and floral and historical exhibitions were th attractions, climaxed by a summer ball.

REV. B.R. KEIR MOILLIET, M.A.
(St. Johns 1930-46)

Rev. Bernard Rambold Keir Moilliet was born in Switzerland, studied Oxford and was ordained at Durham in 1901, before serving in par at Stockton On Tees, Hartlepool and Darlington.

He moved to the Isle of Wight to become Rector of Northwood in but it was six years later in 1930 that he was appointed Vicar of Lo Heath. Rev. Bernard Moilliet was the incumbent through the Secon World War and took an active part in the Boy Scout Movement loc

...hting was an enthusiasm of his and some spare time was given over ...nstructing others in navigation. It was typical of the outdoor nature ...is family and through the summer his four daughters were in the ...it of sleeping out on the vicarage lawn. The said daughters, Rachel, ...da, Faith and Jacqueline all lived at the Vicarage and inevitably the ...ily had a keen interest in the younger generation.

... couple the Moilliets had 'the common touch' and the immensely ...able Mrs. Moilliet would make a habit of rushing around ...ediately upon notifiction of sickness in the parish. She once ...mented that the majority of her time as a Vicar's wife was spent ...bing other people's backs".

...as failing health which forced Bernard Moilliet's retirement in 1946 ...he retired to Wareham. It was a short illness which led to his death ...e in September 1956 and he was survived by his wife.

...ongregations remembered Rev. Keir Moilliet for his ready wit, ...rful humour and in particular for his copious tea-drinking. He was a ...of high ideals and expectations which were not always realised at ...ohns and occasionally led to outbursts of frustration in the parish ...azine. His European extraction made it difficult for him to come to ...s with the typical English reserve of those days.

...vangelical and out-going tendencies meant that he was attracted ...e "Oxford Group" formed by prominent public and clerical figures ...ndon to promote Christianity more vigorously. Bernard Moilliet ...to form a local group but found no sympathisers locally.

...Memorial Services on the deaths of John Robinson and Bernard ...et were held on the same day in September 1956 at 8.45 a.m. ...p.m. respectively at St. John's.

TO: THE MINISTER OF FOOD

25 September 1941

Sir,

Re: Jam

This centre has made about a ton of jam. You promised that this would be bought. The jam is occupying all available storage space and is in danger of deteriorating through being much too closely packed. However excellent the quality, I am told, there should be plenty of air space between the jars.

Enquiries locally and at Reading have been useless. The official either has no power to act, or else he refers us to some other department. The bad old game of 'red tape' in fact.

It will not help the country if even this small quantity of jam is spoilt. I propose to give your department one more week, after which date I will sell the jam locally, before it goes bad.

I hope this will meet with your unofficial (i.e. real) approval, even if officially you have to prosecute me for doing my best for this country. I would be proud to go to prison for such a cause. I should take full responsibility on myself. I still hope however that you may induce your underlings to get a move on.

I am, Sir, yours faithfully,

Rev. B.R. Keir Moilliet

LIL'S STORY
(by Lily Warmington)

After having moved into the area to Abshot Road in 1939 I spent the war years working part-time on a strawberry plot in Warsash Road, li so many others, preparing the ground, planting and then the non-sto picking.

I had always been interested in music, having played the piano and violin as a youngster and in an orchestra in Southsea at the age of 2 had been going to some services at St. John's during war-time and a neighbour Doug Hillman, who was playing the organ at weddings a Johns at the time, took me under his wing and showed me how to p I also travelled to Portsmouth to have lessons on a formal basis at St Luke's and learnt from John Davison who was the organist at Portsmouth Cathedral.

Initially I was in the choir at St. John's but in January 1947 I took ove from a Mrs. Bristow as organist for Rev. Frank Aker. I look back now a position which lasted for 45 years in all, until 1992 when I forced retire through illness. By my counting I have served the Lord in Lock Heath with eight Vicars in all.

I played at two services per Sunday on average over the years, but i often stretched to three to include a baptism. Under Bruce Carpent we held services at Brookfield School at 11 a.m. and that meant ser at 9 a.m. and 6.30 p.m. at St. Johns and the additional service at th school where I played the piano.

The only drawback was that I was forced to hear Bruce preach the sermon at all three services - not that he ever heard me complain!

call that initially my pay was at the rate of £40 per annum with a £1
a for weddings, but most of the money was spent by me on music
ets and hymn books for the choir.

two years I had the responsibility of choosing the psalms and hymns
organising carol services. The biggest change in my time has been
liturgy - for years psalms with chants were a regular part of the
ices such as Matins and Evensong. Bruce Carpenter brought the
jest changes with communion being celebrated three times per
day. Now I am used to new hymns and songs from "Mission Praise"
even the introduction of electric keyboards as accompaniment.

new informal ways of modern times took some getting used to. For
s nobody used christian names in conversation and everybody called
other "Mr. or Mrs." and it was Bruce Carpenter who first called
'Lil", much to my surprise.

outstanding memories over the years are painful ones! Many years
my husband and I were cycling to church on Christmas Eve for the
night Service and carelessly got tangled up with each other. We
fell off our cycles and I had to climb back on and cycle to church
olay the organ with an injured thumb.

cent Christmas brought another accident when before the late
noon Crib Service for children I fell over in church and broke my
bone. I heard a crack and thought I had broken my glasses. I
d for that service in some pain before going to hospital but missed
est of the Christmas services.

olay regularly at the 11 a.m. service on the 1st Sunday in the month
n other odd occasions as required. I would like to play on to the
unday in January 1997 to record 50 years at the organ at St. John's.

ST. JOHN'S CHURCH

The First 50 Years - A Record of Events

1886	A Tea and Concert Committee raised £150 for the building of a Mission Hall.
1887	Rev. Mills Robbins was in charge under the Vicar of Hook-With-Warsash. Clergy officiating: H.W. Bull, C.L. Perry, R. Burton, G. Pratt, and R. W. Nevill.
February 1893	Locks Heath created as an Ecclesiatical District
16 April 1893	Annual Easter Vestry Meeting in St. John's Mission Room. Vicar's Churchwarden and people's warden elected.
1 June 1893	T. A. M. Archer Shepherd licensed as Minister by Dr. Thorold, Bishop of Winchester. Services held in the Mission School.
24 June 1894	Foundation Stone laid by Augusta Bradshaw, niece of Mrs. Hornby who left the money for both the building and endowing of the church at £150 per annum.
17 August 1895	The church consecrated by Dr. Awdry, Bishop of Southampton. By the Act of Consecration Locks Heath became an Ecclesiastical Parish, under the provisions of the New Parishes Act. The Minister became Vicar and the Church was licensed for marriages. The Mission Hall then became the Church of England Day School.
16 November 1904	First Confirmation Service by Dr. Macarthur, Bishop of Southampton, with 38 confirmed - 23 from Sarisbury, 13 from Locks Heath.
13 July 1906	Dedication of organ by Dr. Macarthur. Organ built by J. Burton of Winchester - Cost £357.
29 September 1907	Last instalment on organ paid to J. Burton.
17 May 1908	Rev. Archer-Shepherd collapsed and died in the vestry whilst robing for the Evening Service.
1908	Two stained-glass windows placed on north wall of chancel. One to memory of Rev. Archer Shepherd, the other to memory of Mrs. Grew, of Highlands, Locks Heath
13 October 1908	The new Vicar, The Rev. Brent R.R. Neville was instituted by the Bishop of Winchester at Farnham
27 October 1908	Rev. Brent Neville was inducted by the Archdeacon of Winchester at Locks Heath.
1 November 1908	Rev. Brent Neville read the 39 Articles.
15 February 1909	Dedication of two stained glass windows, one to the memory of the late Vicar, and the other to Mrs. Grew a late parishioner, by the Archdeacon of Winchester.
25 April 1909	Confirmation by Bishop of Southampton of 32 candidates from the parish. Service was at 3 pm on Sunday afternoon with the church being crowded with 500 present. The Bishop remained for the Evening Service and preached - again were 500 present.

28 July 1909	A Garden Fete and Sale of Work was held in the Park, Locks Heath in aid of the decoration, ventilation, lighting of the church. The fete was opened the first day by Mrs. Arthur Lee and the second by Mrs. Babington. The amount taken during the two days amounted to £125.
May 1910	A Memorial Service in commemoration of his late Majesty King Edward V11 was held in the church at 2.30 p.m. and the Vicar gave an address.
0	Church painted and decorated in two colours, terracotta and light green with fleur de Lis, with ventilators in the roof being added.
1911	Lantern Services were held in the church on Thursday evenings during Lent drawing congregations of 400-500.
June 1911	A United Coronation Service was held in the church at 3 p.m. after the service at Westminster Abbey. Coronation mugs were given to the children in memory of the Coronation of their Majesties King George and Queen Mary.
January 1912	A Church Army Van Mission was held in the parish from 23 January to 8 February. The meetings were well attended.
ber 1913	Acting under urgent medical advice the Vicar Rev. Brent Neville accepted a chaplaincy abroad during the winter months, he returned but had to retire eventually. The Rev. H.E. Henekey acted as Locum Tenens during his absence.
26 April 1915	Induction and Institution of Rev. J.C. Robinson
11 December 1915	Preliminary meeting unanimously agrees to form a Church Council to assist the Vicar and Church Wardens.
1 January 1916	Parochial Church Council met for the first time. - agree to form a Poor Fund Committee. Main item concerns water in church accumulating in stokehole with damage to church and organ. First secretary to the P.C.C. was Col. Brewster.
May 1918	A scheme for a Parish Room, subsequently developed as a Memorial Hall, was embarked on.
30 March 1921	Report from choir meeting received by P.C.C. Report considered to be 'irregular and offensive'. A Vote of Confidence in the Vicar passed.
14 February 1922	Memorial Hall opened.
11 June 1922	Memorial screen in church dedicated.
15 January 1924	For the first time ever PCC report that 'in view of state of finances it is impossible to pay any of our quota for the past year'.
11 October 1924	Consecration of new cemetery by Bishop of Southampton
March 1925	William Frank Cooper deceased, formerly a sidesman at St. John's, occupied the first adult grave at new St. John's Road Burial Ground.
1926	Major repairs to organ necessary. Damage to church roof caused by big tree falling on it.

November 1926	Severe problem obtaining coke or anthracite for church, due to coal strike.
22 October 1928	Death of Mrs. Robinson, the Vicar's wife.
March 1930	Electric light installed in the church and Memorial Hall, with Mrs. Archer-Shepherd as the benefactor. Reredos and Wood Panelling installed in the Sanctuary of the church. The former given by Rev. J.C. Robinson in memory of his wife Nina Arnier Robinson and the latter by her friends. A credence table was installed as a gift of the Mothers Union and a silver gilt wafer box also in her memory by the Winchester Women Messengers.
3 December 1930	Agreement to form classes for purpose of education in church history 'in view of modern scientific developments'.
22 January 1931	Proposal to provide water to Vicarage - estimate £24. Urgent 'as Vicar and family have to do their own pumping and the well-water was not fit for drinking purposes'. Scheme to provide Vicarage with electric light - estimate £22.
14 April 1931	Agreed that choir boys be paid - 1d for each practice attended.
25 February 1931	Induction of Rev. B.R.K. Moilliet as Vicar on Rev. Robinson's retirement.
May 1932	Considerable expenditure on Church school agreed - estimate for repairs to roof and playground - £56.
May 1934	Installation of electric blower to organ agreed - estimate £81.
Summer 1937	Future of church school debated. Faced with considerable expenditure for draining and resurfacing playground - estimate £277. If funds not raised Education Authority would take over the school. PCC voted to raise the funds - 'undesirable to give up school'.
January 1938	Approach from St. John the Baptist, Rife, Albert Canada for funds for resident minister to be appointed. Voted to give proceeds of collection Sunday nearest to Patronal Festival each year.
July 1938	A piece of masonry (Norman, about 1100 A.D.) from St. Peter's, Titchfield was fixed to the North Wall of church.
August 1940	Leaflet issued during war-time, instead of parish magazine.
July 1941	A jam-making centre at church made about one ton of jam for Ministry of Food, which was subsequently not collected and had to be thrown away.
May 1943	Gift of £16 presented to Mr. Lambden to mark 40 years service as church verger, sexton and c
December 1943	Thriving youth club reported - 75 members en; drama, choral, talks, dancing and football.

| February 1944 | Joint Petition and proposal from St. Johns and Congregational churches to approach Fareham Urban District Council to make Locks Heath into a separate ward, instead of being divided up between three neighbouring wards. 1102 signatures obtained from 528 houses protesting at the "mutilation of Locks Heath parish". |

September 1944 50th annniversary of church foundation celebrated at Garden Party with tea, and re-enactment of scenes from the preceding years Rev. Keir Moilliet remembered the "benefactors of this church… who gave services of a personal rather than material sort, Charlotte Hornby, Augusta Bradshaw, Henry Bradshaw, Gladys Paget, Caroline Archer Shepherd, Thomas Archer Meynell Shepherd, Women Messengers, J. C. Robinson, Jyoti Nand, William Green, Emily Horsfall and Wilfred Rapley. "

A CENTURY OF Worship

PART TWO - THE LAST 50 YEARS

Century of Worship
HE ST JOHN'S CHURCH STORY
art Two

The Parish's Existence Under Threat

er the war the Church school continued to require a significant
ount of management and financing and in May 1949 the Parish
rch Council reluctantly agreed to convert the school to "controlled"
us.

hen Rev. Bernard Moilliet had retired and been replaced by the Rev.
k Aker in 1946. His incumbency was clouded by the continued
ussion in the diocese over the possible amalgamation of his parish
that at nearby Titchfield for "economic reasons". Much effort was
nded during the last years of his tenure on constructing a case for
s Heath to continue as a separate parish but before a decision was
Frank Aker had retired on health grounds. Subsequently he put
aching skills to good use by opening a private junior school in the
e.

the future of the parish in the early 50s was racked with
rtainty as the Bishop and the Diocese considered the union
ns. For almost eighteen months St. John's had to make do with a
In Charge in the form of the Vicar of Titchfield, the Rev. Norman

event the Parish Church Council was relieved to be notified in
st 1955 that the Bishop had decided that the union of the parishes
onsidered to be unworkable.

9. A New Vicar has to Rebuild

This decision enabled the new incumbent Rev. Edwin Curtis to press on
to rebuild the parish's morale. As evidence of this Christmas 1958
marked the end of a major two-year exercise in fund-raising for the cost
of essential restoration of the church building. Re-roofing, re-tiling and
renewal of the drains and guttering throughout were the major items of
work which could be commenced as a result.

The management and financing of the Memorial Hall were heavy
burdens for the Church Council. The Village Community Association
had taken over control at a minimum rent in 1964 but the Council were
happy to sell the Hall the following year to the Fareham Council.

10. Bruce Carpenter Heralds a New Era

When the Edwin Curtis was tempted to move to the islands of
Mauritius and the Seychelles as their Bishop his replacement Rev. Bruce
Carpenter moved just a few miles down the road from St. Peter and St.
Paul, Fareham.

The arrival in the 60s of Bruce Carpenter heralded a period of
innovation and changes in the patterns of worship and outreach at St.
John's.

His "Street Link Scheme" bound the parish together and was a
trailblazer for the now long-established "Communicare" organisation.

Bruce Carpenter's commitment even extended to organising a special
additional Sunday service at Sarisbury Secondary School to meet the
needs of parishioners at the boundary edges.

During his stay a Garden of Rest was established, and in church a new Side Altar was consecrated and sound amplifying equipment was installed.

Always active in the community Bruce Carpenter played a full part in discussions surrounding the controversial plans to extensively develop the area. He was a vocal executive member of the Solent Plan Society whose brief was to represent the views of the local population to the planners.

When Bruce moved to Holy Trinity, Fareham after an eventful 7-year stay he had seen a great surge in not only the size of the parish population due to the frenzied property development but also the congregation.

His influence is still felt in the way that the Eucharist forms the centre-point of our Sunday worship, in the way that the church is represented on many community ventures such as the Day Centre, Youth Concern and Abbeyfield Society, and in the way that a family service is a long-established fixture.

11. A Disastrous Appointment and a Welcome Replacement

The short six-month stay of the Rev. Derek Nicholls coincided with the completion of the much-discussed re-organisation of the chancel, the planning for which had started during Bruce Carpenter's time. The main constituent was the forward moving of the altar close to the chancel steps. After the hurried departure of Rev. Derek Nicholls St. John's was pleased to welcome Rev. Norman Chatfield from Sandown on the Isle of Wight. When, for the first time, a full-time Assistant Curate was

appointed at St. John's it necessitated the purchase by the diocese of a residence at Laurel Road in the parish for the Rev. Michael Sheffield and his wife.

Amongst all the plans for the development of the area and the provision of appropriate facilities was the construction of an ecumenic centre for use by all denominations and located on the site of the future district centre. Any thoughts and plans for a new hall were put on ho as a consequence. In the end the proposal was abandoned and the church were left to maintain and improve the existing hall.

12. A Sad Goodbye to Norman, a Big Hallo to Bob

When Norman Chatfield moved to Alverstoke as Rector in November 1982 the parish welcomed Rev. Bob Evens, formerly the curate at St. Mary's in Portchester, as their new Vicar the following summer. He w soon supplemented by the Rev. Michael Lloyd as curate, following the earlier departure of his predecessor Rev. Michael Sheffield.

The development of the Fareham Western Wards continued without respite and the size of the congregations through the 80s reflected the massive growth of the population and the warm charismatic natu of Bob Evens' ministry.

Under his influence there was more emphasis on external giving with the institution of the "Focus" scheme whereby various charities were nominated for fund-raising in designated periods through the year.

Jane Richards became a Reader in 1980 followed by Jenny Lowater following year as ladies began to take ministry roles at St. John's. It in 1985 that the first tentative moves towards a new Church Hall to place when a small task-group met to specify the requirements.

creased emphasis on the Eucharist as the focal point for worship
e installation of an evening communion service in 1986 and by
ere was no place for either Matins or Evensong which for so
ears were the main morning and evening services. In addition
mily Service had become a monthly feature.

n's was well represented on the Locks Heath Day Centre Group
Bullen and also on a working party which concerned itself with
vision of youth facilities in the area.

Momentous Decision and a Huge Commitment

in 1988 that the congregation courageously set out on the path
s the building of a new Church Hall and Extension. Much prayer
art-searching went into the decision and an equal amount of
ork on fund-raising. Bob and Sue Evens and their young family
give up the pleasure of living in the original old Vicarage and
o a new home so that it could be sold and developed and the
found for the necessary extra car-parking spaces.

congregation celebrated the 100th Anniversary of the
ration of the Church in 1895 so the new Church Centre began to
t. They had prayed for God's guidance over the previous ten
nd successive Church Councils had re-affirmed its belief that it
od's will that the Centre be built.

HEATING

It was in June 1946 that the congregation had the good news that the Church Council had decided to instal a new heating system. Estimates showed that the new system involved a boiler, to be housed outside the south wall in a stokehold together with low pressure hot water apparatus including radiators and pipes around the church.

Messrs. Lankester and Sons, of Southampton, installed the system before the winter and the cost fell just short of £500. The Council already had about £250 in a Heating Fund and the balance had to be largely raised from the annual Day of Offering that year.

AMALGAMATION OF THE PARISHES OF TITCHFIELD AND LOCKS HEATH?
July 1952

At a Special General Meeting of Church Members a Resolution and Memorandum was passed unanimously as follows - " That the amalgamation of the parishes of Titchfield and Locks Heath, as proposed by the Diocesan Pastoral Committee, would be detrimental to the Church, and that a copy of the following memorandum be sent to the Rural Dean for presentation to the Committee".

Extracts from the MEMORANDUM

"The General Meeting of the parishioners of Locks Heath begs to draw the attention of the Committee to the following points:-

1. The parishioners of Locks Heath are prepared to augment the stipend of the incumbent, on the avoidance of the benefice, and the institution of a successor, provided he be Vicar of Locks Heath only, to £550 per year net.

2. Locks Heath parish is an urban area of growing population (2500 adults) which number will increase rapidly during the next few years when the new oil refinery is developed and its employees need housing. 200 houses are scheduled for the next five years.

3. Communicants at Locks Heath have increased by almost 60% in the last few years. Deterioration would be inevitable with decreased opportunities for Holy Communion.

4. Locks Heath has always fulfilled its commitments to the Diocese completely.

5. Locks Heath does not receive financial help from the Diocese in any way.

6. Locks Heath, after a long struggle, has only just become a unit in the civil sense, and is now a ward. It would be a great pity to break up this hard-won unity.

7. The well-known insular character of the Titchfield-born parishioners would make any joint efforts singularly difficult.

In the event the congregation of St. Johns had to wait in limbo for three years , sharing a vicar, Rev. Norman Miller, with St. Peter's of Titchfield, before the Diocese announced that their representations had been accepted and the powers that be conceded that the propsals were "unworkable".

REV. FRANK PRICE AKER B.A.
(St. Johns 1946-55)

Rev. Frank Aker was born in 1908 and secured his B.A degree at th University of London before studying theology at the College of th Resurrection, Mirfield near Leeds. He was ordained in 1932 by the Bishop of Salisbury and was a curate for three years at Blandford F before becoming Vicar in Whitwell, Norfolk for thirteen years.

Rev. Frank Aker arrived in Locks Heath, with his distinctive monocl successor to the retiring Rev. Moilliet in March 1946 and the Vicara was occupied by the family of four, his wife being accompanied by two children Nicholas then aged seven and Jennifer (nicknamed Bu aged five.

During the period whilst the question of merging the Locks Heath Titchfield parishes was under consideration Frank Aker had to shar ministry at St. John's with Rev. Norman Miller from Titchfield. As p an unsatisfactory arrangement it was generally agreed that in the of either retiring the other would assume sole control of both paris

As it transpired Frank Aker was forced to retire through ill-health ir 1955 and then opened a private fee-paying school in the village. In event the merger plan was scrapped by the diocese eventually.

St. Johns was to be his last post in charge of a parish and he spent fifteen years subsequently officiating in various parishes in the Portsmouth area to help out. He retired to Badminton in Glouceste where he died in 1971 at the age of 63.

Rev. Frank Aker with the youngsters in his day-school (c. 1950)

GARDEN OF REMEMBRANCE

For many years the garden has been cared for by George Pink and his family. George was responsible for the creation of the garden when he asked in 1967 for an area of land to be set aside so that the ashes of his son Graham could be placed locally. Since then the garden has also accomodated the ashes of George's wife Celia.

By 1989 the Garden was full and it was no longer possible for individual stones to be placed there. It was decided to set aside a walled area with a flower bed in which ashes could be interred.

Now the names of the deceased are recorded in a Book of Remembrance kept in church in a locked cabinet on permanent display. The pages are turned daily to reflect the anniversaries of the deceased on the exact date.

REV. ERNEST EDWIN CURTIS, BSC., O.B.E
(St. Johns 1955-66)

Rev. Edwin Curtis, born in 1906, studied at Wells Theological College and was a curate at Waltham Cross (1933-36), in Mauritius (1937-44) and at Portsea (1944-47) before becoming the Vicar of All Saints and St. Wilfrid's in Portsmouth. During the latter period he served as the Chaplain of the Royal Portsmouth Hospital. Edwin Curtis was installed as incumbent at St. John's in December 1955 and succeeded Frank A on his retirement. In the interim period the parish had been served by Rev. Norman Miller, the Vicar of Titchfield.

Edwin Curtis's stay in Locks Heath included a tragic episode when during a family holiday in Scotland in the Shetlands they were involved in a road accident in which his wife was killed. Edwin himself suffered serious injuries and spent some weeks in hospital in Scotland before being flown back to a hospital in the South, with the cost being met the P.C.C.

Edwin Curtis is remembered as an intellectual and a preacher whose sermons had great depth and meaning even if some lesser minds struggled to absorb the meanings.

Older parishioners acknowledge that the incumbency of Edwin Curtis marked a period when for the first time there was 'open house' at the Vicarage. His residence became available for meetings and everybody was welcome to drop in. His caring nature was typified by his annual gesture of finding a child in the village whose family did not have the means to take him or her on holiday and offer to take the child away with his own family.

was to be eleven years after his arrival that Edwin Curtis left Locks
...ath for the Seychelles to take up an appointment as the Bishop of
...uritius and the Seychelles in November 1966. He was consecrated at
...eremony at Canterbury Cathedral by the Archbishop of Canterbury
... seventy of his parishioners from St. Johns were there to support him.

...arrival in Mauritius Bishop Curtis unexpectedly found the diocese in
...ate of virtual bankruptcy. When the news of his distress reached this
...ntry funds for the diocese were allocated from the Bishop of
...smouth's annual Appeal.

...l a new Vicar was appointed in his place at St. John's it was
...ounced that Rev. Ted Royds-Jones , who had been his assistant for
...e time after his retirement from a teaching position at Price's School
...areham, would be in charge of the parish.

...n Edwin Curtis arrived in Mauritius he met up again with a former
...ber of his congregation at St. Johns. Evelyn Josling had left Locks
...h in 1968 to work as a missionary in Africa but eventually the
...ion with Edwin led to their marriage in Mauritius. It was his second
...iage after his first wife's tragic death in Scotland.

...n Curtis was elevated to the position of Archibishop of the Indian
...n in 1972. On his retirement in 1976 he returned to this country,
...awarded the O.B.E, and carried out some part-time work in the
...diocese as Assistant Bishop of Portsmouth before moving to Ryde
...e Isle of Wight.

...n Curtis approaches his 90th birthday in poor health at present.

REV. BRUCE LEONARD HENRY CARPENTER, B.A.

(St. Johns 1967-74)

Bruce Carpenter was born in 1932 in Ryde, Isle of Wight, grew up there and his friends would tease him about his "island accent". After leaving school he studied French and Spanish at the Sorbonne, Paris before joining the Royal Navy. At one time Bruce was a Russian interpreter in the senior service but after deciding to join the clergy, Bruce trained at the Durham Theological College. It was in 1959 that he took up his first post as curate in Portsmouth at St. Mark's, North End (1959-63). A similar position in Fareham at St. Peter and Paul (1963-67) followed before Bruce Carpenter moved to Locks Heath as Vicar.

Bruce was married on 1 April 1967, at the Church of St. Peter and St. Paul in Fareham, to Angela ten days before his induction at St. John's. Forty members of the congregation at St. John's were there to greet their new vicar and his young wife. Later their family was completed by the birth of Joanna, one year later by Nicholas and finally by Teresa in 1973.

Angela was a teacher at grammar schools in Fareham and her father, Rev. D. H. Mortimer, was Vicar of Lytchett Minster in Dorset. She shared her husband's love of singing and joined the Locks Heath Ladies Choir.

During the interregnum before his arrival the parish had been in the care of Rev. Ted Royds-Jones, after the departure of Edwin Curtis. In a hugely influential seven-year stay Bruce Carpenter was responsible for introducing the 'Street Link Scheme' begun one year after he arrived and brought from his previous church in Fareham. The Scheme went from strength to strength and eventually became the popular and thriving 'Communicare' organisation, acquiring its own minibus.

Initially the pattern of services was maintained i.e. a said Communion 8 a.m., the Parish Communion (Sung) at 9 a.m. with a Parish Breakfast afterwards, the 'Family' Service at 11 a.m., followed by the Evensong 6.30 p.m.

In his first message to his new congregation Bruce Carpenter was adamant - "I regard the Sung Parish Communion as the chief meeting point of the faithful Christians of the parish. The ideal, as I see it, is one service, of the one whole Christian family, gathered round the Lord's table and offering the Eucharist with all the beauty, dignity and since we can. I must say straight away that I shall expect every committed Christian at St. John's to attend the Parish Communion every week if is humanly possible. The 8 a.m. said service is basically intended as an extra chance for those who cannot get to the 9 a.m. service. The 11 a.m. Family Service is really a children's service and Evensong, although it is a beautiful service, is really just a monastic service of Vespers, blown up into a piece of public worship. It is not on the same plane at all as the Communion and it doesn't fulfil our Lord's command to his disciples 'Do this in remembrance of Me'."

Bruce was the instigator of parish parties to build fellowship, of parish retreats and of a monthly Evening Communion Service. He was a hard worker in the cause of links with other churches and his ecumenical programme "Nine for Christ" was evidence of his belief in church unity.

Strong and hard-hitting views often came from Bruce Carpenter and was never more controversial than when in a parish magazine article described Jesus as "dark-skinned, coloured, of a different race from a wog if you like", The article which received extensive Press coverage was attacking the "completely irrational" beliefs of some Christians o accepted the religion of Jesus Christ, and yet could not accept se who were of another race or colour, as He was. The resulting troversy led Bruce to arrange discussion groups in the parish to uss the racial problem.

Links Scheme demonstrated that to Bruce Carpenter the mmunity' was vitally important and that you didn't have to be a ular churchgoer in order to win a place in his fully committed time.

extra Sunday morning service at Sarisbury Secondary School, as it known then, was also an innovative feature he introduced. Bruce's al coincided with a rapid growth in the parish population, notably ried couples up to age 40 with young children.

e Carpenter had meant so much to Locks Heath during his 7 year and equally when he left the parish he admitted that it was with a avy heart". In a last message to his congregation he said - "I have n wondered if there is a parish priest in England as fortunate as I in terms of support and friendship from both the church gregation and the residents of the parish".

e at St. John's Bruce Carpenter became Rural Dean of Fareham and ort but his next appointment in October 1974 saw him return to ham to Holy Trinity, with St. Columba, as Team Rector (1974-84). ob involved overseeing two churches and five clergy in a parish of 00 and he also became Honorary Canon at Portsmouth Cathedral.

e's next appointment took him away from the district to Richmond car at St. Mary's (1984-91). In 1991 he moved to Ashford in Kent to up a position as Teaching Chaplain in a new church high-school, ucting in French and Religious Education. Now Bruce is also bringing rceful but kindly character to his parish ministry at Ashford.

Bruce and Angela Carpenter with Joanna, Nicholas and baby Teresa

A SAD CHAPTER

When Rev. Bruce Carpenter left St. Johns in 1974 with many sad farewells he was always going to be a hard act to follow for his successor. It has to be recorded however that the appointment of Rev.Derek Nicholls was not a success and that had nothing to do with his successor's influence.

From soon after his induction in March 1975 it became obvious to the congregation that Derek Nicholls was wholly unsuited to the incumbency and that, coupled with his personal problems, meant that his early resignation and departure from the Vicarage and the Anglican priesthood six months later was inevitable.

Happily St. John's was able to quickly forget their unfortunate experience and enjoy the ministry of his immediately-popular successor in the form of Norman Chatfield.

EDIE GROVE - EVER FAITHFUL

(A tribute by Rev Jane Richards)

It would be true to say that Edie belonged to St. John's all her life, following in the footsteps of her family, other than a period when she worked away from home as a nanny.

The church family became her family - she was "Auntie Edie" to Bruce Carpenter's children and regularly babysat for them.

Her major contribution to St. John's during her lifetime was as sacristan, involving as it did organising the vestry, taking responsibility for the a linen, together with the sanctuary and chancel cleaning.

The job was carried out for years with meticulous care and attention detail. Heaven help anybody in Edie's vestry who was unable to tell th difference between a pyx and a purificator. If you were willing to lear Edie was a marvellous teacher.

Only the very best was good enough for the worship of God was Ed motto and her unseen ministry, taken for granted by most people, enabled that worship.

Edie walked from her house next to Plessey's to St. John's on a daily basis and for years she was the only lay person to join the clergy for morning and evening prayer each day and her faithfulness was a tremendous support to them.

On a Saturday she was in church by 4 p. m. to prepare for the next day's services and that day's Evensong at 6 p. m. She would attend every main service on Sundays and vigorously rang the bell immedia after the consecration at Communion.

Edie did not suffer fools gladly, in the vestry she terrorised the slopp the careless, and she certainly had a bark! But for all that she was a immensely kind and caring, and her faith filled her life.

On her death Edie left her whole estate to St. John's, and her gener has been a major factor in the decision to build the church centre. I think of her every time I prepare the vessels for Communion - and g thanks for her.

EV. NORMAN CHATFIELD, B.A., M.A.

. Johns 1976-83)

man Chatfield was born in 1937 and graduated from Ripon Hall,
ord. He took up his first post in 1962 as curate at Burgess Hill and
n at Uckfield before becoming Vicar at St. Joseph's in Sandown on
sle of Wight in 1969.

as seven years later that he moved to Locks Heath in 1976 and
ed for almost seven years. Norman is best remembered for
loping the prayer life of the parish in his quiet unassuming fashion,
h also was the hallmark of his unstinting non-public pastoral
stry. Plans for the new District Centre, with considerable discussion
t a possible ecumenical church centre therein, came and went, and
pied much of Norman's time and efforts. Similarly plans for
lding the church hall and the extension or re-ordering of the
ch itself were never finalised and inevitably finance was at the root
e frustrated aims.

ng his incumbency Norman introduced the Reservation of the
ment for the Sick and completed the re-organisation of the
cel which Bruce Carpenter had begun. Numerous community links
established by Norman and he was anxious to encourage the
th of lay ministry, the seeds of which had been laid by his
cessor.

cumbency was marked by considerable growth in the social life of
nurch. Work with children and young people assumed a greater
tance and much of Norman's plans revolved around the expected
sion in the population. Ironically Locks Heath's development only

took off after his departure but his successor Bob Evens benefited from
much of the groundwork laid by Norman.

The quiet but popular vicar had a zany sense of humour which regularly
surfaced with a joke in the weekly brieflet.

Norman Chatfield's next appointment was as Rector at St. Mary's
Alverstoke and during that incumbency he was Chaplain at both
H.M.Prison, Haslar and Gosport War Memorial Hospital.

After eight years at Alverstoke Norman left to take up a post as Canon
at Gloucester Cathedral in 1991 where he still serves currently.

*Rev. Norman Chatfield with his wife Janet and family, from left, Matthew,
Elizabeth and Rebecca*

REV. ROBERT J.S. EVENS
(1983-)

Bob, our present Vicar, was born in Plymouth and attended schools in Devon, Kent and Dorset before taking his first job as a bank clerk in Bristol. After nine years and a professional banking qualification to his credit Bob left the world of finance and commenced studying theology at Trinity College in Bristol. Three years later, following his ordination, Bob took up a post as curate at St. Simon's in Southsea (1977-79) at age of 30.

A curacy at St. Mary's in Portchester followed (1979-83) until Bob became our Vicar in 1983.

By now Bob had been married to Sue, whom he had met when she studying for a law degree at Bristol University. At the time of their m to Locks Heath to succeed Rev. Norman Chatfield Bob and Sue were parents of Thomas (three) and Claire (eight months). Bob is a sailing enthusiast with caravanning as a recent holiday pursuit and interest.

Since 1993 Bob has also served as Rural Dean of Fareham and in 19 was elected as a member of the General Synod.

OB'S MINISTRY AT ST. JOHN'S

Personal reflection by Rev. Anne Boggust

as on July 3rd 1983 that Bob and Sue arrived in a very hot and
ny Locks Heath. From that day on Bob was anxious that St. Johns
uld be a truly "parish" church where everyone in the village could
a welcome and be enabled to worship.

of Bob's first areas of concern was for the families with young
dren and within a few weeks of his arrival a creche was established ,
by a rota of mothers in the church hall, during the Sunday morning
ice.

n this early concern has grown today's Youth Council which
dinates all the groups who meet either on Sundays or during the
k for activities or teaching - from babies right through to the
agers at college. By these groups meeting on three Sundays per
th and a Family Service for all on the other Sunday parents and
ren are enabled to come to the communion rail together to receive
s blessing.

of Bob's innovations was to ensure that he was in the porch prior
e 9.30 a.m. Sunday service so that he could meet people as they
ed. By this means Bob had the opportunity not only to meet
omers but to get to know their names so that later during the
e he could give people communion on a more personal basis by
their christian names.

uilt on a service pattern already established but early in his
try he used a questionnaire to obtain the views of the
regation on what they wanted from the service they attended.

From these views arose the significant change from the long-established
Evensong to a service of Holy Communion at 6.30 p.m.

Since inception this evening communion has matured over the years to
a quiet reflective service valued by many. The service gives the
opportunity three times per year for the laying on of hands for healing.

In 1988 it was decided to give over one service per month to Evening
Praise- a non-communion service of a flexible nature with the accent on
praise music in the modern idiom.

In recent years the Family Service at 9.30 a.m. on the first Sunday has
been followed by a sung Book of Common Prayer communion service
at 11 a.m.

In 1992 a Morning Worship service was introduced successfully on a
non-communion basis with the emphasis on teaching contained in a
20-minute spot.

At each stage there has been full consultation which has enabled
change and growth to be prayerfully undertaken. Similarly when
planning for buildings to accommodate future growth this has been
very apparent.

The early years of Bob's ministry coincided with a vast population
explosion in the Western Wards and he soon realised that a bold
approach to the future needs of St. John's and the parish was required.
From 1985, when an architect was appointed, plans for a much larger
hall than originally envisaged were drawn up together with the addition
of a three-storey church centre and a possible gallery.

In the event it transpired that Bob and Sue had to leave the old vicarage
which had been their home so that it might be sold by the diocese to

provide the funds to enable land to be acquired for the provision of the required car-parking spaces. Now the new hall has been put to good use for nearly four years and the Church Centre at the west end started.

In addition Bob has been a most effective "trainer" for newly-ordained clergy and four full-time curates have come under his wing - Michael Lloyd in 1984, Stuart Holt in 1987, Jonathan Watson in 1990 and now David Weir newly ordained in 1995.

During Bob's tenure vocations from the parish have grown. Jenny Lowater and Jane Richards have been ordained as priests, and Anne Boggust as a deacon. Matthew Thomson has been ordained deacon this year and is serving elsewhere in the diocese. Currently there are three more non-stipendiary ministers in training from St. John's.

The sharing of ministry encouraged by Bob has led to two members of the congregation being called to be lay readers, with another three in training currently. At his instigation teams of people are now involved in such areas as Baptism preparation, welcome group, bereavement support and the Friendly Faces team of "listening ears", to name but a few.

A recent feature of St. John's has been the increased involvement of music in worship. The choir together with music groups and instrumental accompaniment have been encouraged. This has enabled many to offer their talents in the musical field to the glory of God.

Many have appreciated the social life of the church - barn dances, barbecues, rambles, treasure hunts etc., together with the annual retreat, and such events have been built on to enable everyone, including newcomers, to feel welcomed and valued,

In recent times Bob's ministry has extended to the Fareham Deanery by his appointment as Rural Dean. Here again his skill in encouraging

people has enabled the deanery to draw closer together. In 1994 he was elected to the General Synod to fill a vacancy which has put him touch with national church affairs.

Holding together a worshipping community of over 500 people at St. John's with unity and love has been no easy task, and Bob will rightly say that it has been a team effort - but every team needs a leader

Like his modern predecessors Norman Chatfield and Bruce Carpenter Bob believes that the way to get people into the Kingdom of God is love them, and how blessed the people of St. John's and Locks Heath have been to be the recipients of such a loving and inspirational ministry, all with the support of his family of Sue, Tom and Claire.

The "Team" (c. 1990) from left George Cutcher, Jane Richards, Bob Evens Jonathan Watson and John Nicholls

CARS DECIDE ON ROLE REVERSAL

en Canon John Maybury decided at the age of 60 in the autumn of
91 to move towards retirement he became curate to the vicar who
been his curate at St. Simon's Church in Southsea in the 1970's.
left his post as Vicar at Holy Rood, Stubbington after 13 years and
his wife Beverley bought a retirement bungalow at Titchfield
mmon.

Rood had been a busy parish and in 1991 Rev. Bob Evens at Locks
th suggested John ought to have a quieter life for the sake of his
th and coupled that with the offer of a position as his senior curate.
was attracted by the idea of continuing his ministry in this role in
final years to his normal retirement age, without the pressures of
administration and paper-work.

was that the hard-worked Locks Heath priest found that his new
te was his former boss and their roles had been reversed.

Maybury became a very popular and valuable addition to the St.
's team, and his quiet, knowledgeable and experienced ministry has
of great service to the parish.

John Maybury and Bob Evens find a moment to relax

"BUILDING FOR THE FUTURE"

It was on 22 September 1988 that a Building Liasion Committee was originally set up "to enable the P.C.C. to fulfil its decision to commission a scheme for extension of the church and its facilities, including the Hall".

A Building Executive Committee was established in January 1991 which consisted of both churchwardens, a treasurer, two local builders and a secretary. Terms of reference were agreed by the Church Council and the committee met on a regular basis.

The Project was planned in two phases. Phase 1 was the building of the hall and included preparatory work for Phase 2, which is to extend the west end of the church as a church centre.

Originally a total capital of £610,000 was expected to be required and on the Sunday of 3 March 1991 when the appeal was launched it was announced that £110,000 had already been pledged. The congregation responded to the appeal by giving or promising a further £110,000.

This commitment encouraged the Church Council to proceed with Phase 1 which got under way after a symbolic start to the demolition of the old church hall by the senior churchwarden and the vicar, both suitably attired in overalls and safety helmets.

The inital moneys for Phase 1 were raised by (1) deposited deeds of covenant, (2) regular giving by covenant, (3) fund-raising activities, (4) contributing by way of a tile bucket at the chruch entrance, (5) interest-free loans, (6) gift aid, of £600 or more, and (7) having guarantors to support a bank loan.

The first phase was to build a new Hall and in just over eighteen months the church family gave or loaned over £250,000 to enable the facility to be realised.

When Bishop Timothy came and officially opened the hall on 1 Febru 1992 it was the culmination of Phase 1 in which £250,000 had been given. The hall was immediately brought into daily use. There is now someone in the reception area to welcome people and deal with enquiries, the church secretary works in the office, the Friendly Faces provide a drop-in centre with cups of tea and a listening ear on three afternoons a week, toddlers and their parents enjoy each other's company, and the Fellowship meets for lunch, for talks and for activities.

The hall is also home to study groups, prayer and teaching groups, parties, receptions and social gatherings of every kind. The hall is als let out to local organisations, when available!

On a Sunday morning the hall is crowded as five large groups of childrens meet in the main hall and the attic, and even spill over into the foyer. The choir can be found in the office which serves as their vestry and they often have to hold their final rehearsal in the foyer. Coffee is being made in the kitchen and the congregation come and go, leaving their coats, using the toilet, before going on into church

In 1992 the Church Council found themselves, by design, not meeti their full quota to the Diocese. There was some moral uncertainty within the Council and at an extraordinary meeting in July of that ye was decided at that meeting the quota was more important than a commitment to the building fund and plans for a fund campaign in Autumn 1992 were postponed. In the event the Building Fund

The Bishop of Portsmouth opens the Church Hall in February 1992
In attendance, from left, Jane Richards, Dick Richards, Sheila Stephens, the Bishop, Bob Evens, Jonathan Watson and John Maybury

Campaign for Phase 2 was relaunched in the Autumn of 1994 and revised costings were prepared.

The relaunch had been triggered by the need to replace the church pendant lamps, which was part of Phase 2, and by the approach of St. John's Church centenary year which it was felt would be an excellent focus for the campaign.

At the beginning of January 1995 when it was felt that circumstances permitted the Church Council, on the recommendation of the Building Executive Committee, agreed unanimously to go ahead with Phase 2 of the building project. This involves the contruction of the Church Centre which it was felt was needed to meet the needs of the congregation and the local community.

The new Church Centre at the west end of the church is planned to provide a large ground-floor meeting room. A kitchen is contained within a small envelope which includes the cloakrooms, stairs, entrance area and storage cupboard. On the first floor there will be room for prayer, groups and counselling and on the next floor two more rooms could be used by the clergy and for storage.

An attractive entrance area will serve the centre, with the entrance to the church itself being retained very much in its present form.

More church meetings are planned to take place in the centre during the evenings, thus releasing the hall for use by the wider community.

For the dream to be realised the Council had made it known that £500,000 needed to be pledged and given over the four years involved. After a "Pledge Sunday" in November 1994 the Treasurer Mike Ashley announced that a total of £317,351 had been pledged by way of gifts, current and new interest-free loans, covenants, a tile bucket and a donation from the Church's Legacy Fund.

Initially early contributions had to be committed to a structural survey the west end of the church and the construction of the car park adjacent to the old vicarage.

The building project was to proceed in four stages, namely: (1) sub-structure, foundations and drainage, (2) superstructure and roof, (3) finishing the superstructure and (4) linking the Church Centre to the church. There was a fifth stage to erect a balcony on the west wall to provide more seating but this was postponed until further funds became available.

In the Centenary Year the Parochial Church Council had made what was probably the most momentous decision in its history to go forward with the building project, with the knowledge that it would need an enormous commitment of time, energy and money. The whole enterprise from the start was surrounded with prayer and the church was anxious that God's will be sought at every stage.

The project went forward with faith, with a mission to build a hall and church centre which would give glory to God and enable St. John's serve God's people in Locks Heath for another hundred years. The congregation was aware how much they owed to those who built the sturdy and beautiful church a century ago and were committed to b on that firm foundation.

LOOK HOW WE'RE GROWING!

Electoral Roll (Church membership)

Year	Number	Year	Number
1979	235	1987	365
1980	224	1988	443
1981	229	1989	481
1982	249	1990	495
1983	266	1991	517
1984	236	1992	532
1985	287	1993	518
1986	316	1994	527

John's Churchwardens

/37, 1937/38	W.J. Rew and H. Norton
/39	W.J. Rew and W.A. Norton
/46, 1946/47, /48 and 1948/49	H. Manuel and W.A. Norton
/50	H. Manuel and R. Oakshott
/51, 1951/52	
952/53	P. Peagram and Miss R. Arnold
1953/54 and 1954/55	P. Peagram and W.A. Norton
1955/56, 1956/57, 1957/58, 1958/59	Capt. E.C. Thornton and Dr. E.C. Minors
1959-60, 1960-61, 1961-62 and 1962-63	Dr. E.H. Minors and W.A. Norton
1963-64 and 1964-65	T. Cox and L. Paine
1965-66, 1966-67 and 1967/68	Dr. E.H. Minors and L. Paine
1968/69, 1969/70, 1970/71 and 1971/72	M. Smallwood and A. Jones
1973-4, 1974-5, 1975-76 and 1976-77	R. Knevett and A. Jones
1977-78	R. Knevett and P. Lowater
1978-79 and 1979-80	M.T. Richards and P. Lowater
1980-81, 1981-82	M.T. Richards and P.R. Sherwood
1982-83 and 1983-84	M.T. Richards and P. Lowater
1984-85 and 1985-86	D. Curtis and P. Lowater
1986-87 and 1987-88	D. Curtis and Mrs. A. Boggust
1988-89 and 1989-90	D. Richards and Mrs. A. Boggust
1990-91, 1991-92 and 1992/93	D. Richards and Mrs. S. Stephens
1993/94 and 1994/95	A. Bates and Mrs. S. Stephens
1995 -	Mrs. B. Taylor and J. Ibbotson

VICARS AND CURATES

Vicars		Curates	
1893-08	Rev. T.A.M. Archer Shepherd		
1908-15	Rev. B.R.R. Neville		
1915-31	Rev. J.C. Robinson		
1931-46	Rev. H.K. Moilliet		
1946-54	Rev. F. Aker		
1956-67	Rev. E.E. Curtis		
		1964-72	Rev. E.M. Royds-Jones
1967-74	Rev. B.L.H. Carpenter		
		1973-80	Rev. E.Q. Snook
1975	Rev. D. Nicholls		
1976-82	Rev. N. Chatfield		
1983-	Rev. R.J.S. Evens	1979-83	Rev. M.J. Sheffield
		1984-86	Rev. M.F. Lloyd
		1987-88	Rev. J. Lowater
		1987-90	Rev. S. Holt
		1987-90	Rev. J.V. Richards
		1991-94	Rev. J.R.G Watson
		1991-95	Rev. J.M. Maybury
		1994-	Rev. A. Boggust
		1995-	Rev. D. Weir
		1995	Rev J.V. Richards

Rev. John Maybury (1991-1995)

Rev. Jane Richards (1987-)

. JOHN'S CHURCH

e last 50 years - Record of events

arch 1946	Institution of Rev. Frank Price Aker, B.A. as Vicar by the Bishop of Portsmouth
March 1946	If Church school was to continue on state-aided basis £8000 was needed to bring it 'up to standard'. £4000 available from the Government, £2000 required from each of the Diocese and St. Johns.
May 1946	Estimate of £372 obtained to instal heating urgently in Church- until then coke stoves to be maintained.
ctober 1948	Installation of heating completed. A stoker had to be employed at 15 shillings per week to visit the church three times daily to enable 'gentle heating' to be provided all week.
ay 1949	Agreement to change school to 'Controlled' status - i.e. still church school but no right to appoint teachers. Change effective from 13 February 1950.
y 1952	Pastoral Reorganisation Diocesan Committee suggest Locks Heath and Titchfield be united, with one vicar and vicarage at Titchfield.
ry 1954	Resignation of Rev. F. Aker
arch 1954	Appointment of Rev. N.A.L. Miller (Vicar of Titchfield) as Priest In Charge for two years during which time the Bishop will decide whether Locks Heath should continue as a separate parish or have a union with Titchfield with one Vicar and one Council, for economic reasons.
1 May 1954	Vicarage let for two years to a private tenant during the sequestration.
15 August 1955	Bishop announces to St. Johns P.C.C. that the union of Titchfield and Locks Heath parishes will not proceed as considered to be unworkable.
December 1955	Rev. Edwin Curtis is inducted as Vicar.
December 1958	Service of thanksgiving following re-roofing of church, re-tiling and renewal of drains and guttering. Target of £2236 passed for such church restoration in two years.
November 1959	Church Council resolves to seek and obtain site for a new church to be built for increasing population of parish.
October 1964	Rev. E.M. Royds-Jones takes up post as part-time assistant (on retirement from Price's School Fareham. Community Association take over Memorial Hall from Church Council at nominal rent of £1 per annum - but bingo not permitted by P.C.C.
17 April 1965	Rev. Edwin Curtis signs contract for sale of Memorial Hall to Fareham Council - sale realises £2175 to Diocesan Board of Finance.

January 1967	Departure of Rev. E. Curtis to take up post as Bishop of Mauritius.
14 April 1967	Induction of Rev. Bruce Carpenter by Bishop of Portsmouth May 1967. Sale of corner of churchyard to Fareham Council to enable widening and making-up of Locksheath Park Road.
May 1967	Friday Youth Club started.
21 May 1967	Family Service televised.
October 1967	Part of churchyard set aside for laying of Garden of Rest.
November 1967	Evening service switched to 4 p.m. for winter
7 December 1967	Consecration of new Side Altar by Bishop Noel Chamberlain.
October 1968	Boiler bursts in church and is replaced by oil-fired boiler.
June 1969	75th Anniversary celebrations end with World Fair in aid of missionary work.
July 1969	New Church Hall used for the first time after completion at cost of £3000 from proceeds of sale of Memorial Hall.
July 1969	Street Link and Emergency Transport Schemes launched - network covering 50 streets.
11 October 1970	First service at Sarisbury Secondary School - weekly communion at 11 a.m. (As a consequence Rev. B. Carpenter conducting up to four communions per Sunday).
June 1971	Retirement of Rev. Ted Royds-Jones (Asst. vicar)
June 1971	Summons served upon P.C.C. following dispute with Warsash Construction Co. over cost of building Church Hall.
November 1971	Formation of Locks Heath branch of Abbeyfield Society, with Bishop of Portsmouth as president
March 1972	Ordination of Rev. E.Q. (Jimmy) Snook (former Methodist Minister) as Priest.
September 1972	Bid by Abbeyfield Society for purchase of Vicarage as a home - refused by Diocese.
November 1972	Proposal to instal sound amplifying equipment in Church at cost of c.£200.
January 1973	Jane Taylor becomes first member of St. John's congregation to be accepted for training for women's ministry.
July 1973	Street Link scheme merged into expanded "Communicare" Scheme. Experimental re-planning of chancel.
March 1974	United Church Mission fortnight involving nine churches in the area.

1974	Locks Heath 80th Birthday Festival held-25 organisations take part.
ober 1974	Rev. Bruce Carpenter appointed to head the Team Ministry at Holy Trinity, Fareham. Rev. Jimmy Snook to officiate at all services during interregnum.
ember 1974	Farewell service for the departing Rev. Bruce Carpenter. Reconstructed altar consecrated. (created by boys of Brookfield School under guidance of masters J. Ansell and B. Dale)
ch 1975	Induction of Rev. Derek Edward Nicholls by Bishop of Portsmouth.
1975	Chancel re-organisation completed.

- Reconstruction of existing altar table

- re-alignment of plinth to enable altar to be brought forward near chancel steps

- re-positioning of choir stalls and altar rails

- removal of wooden pulpit on stone base

- tinting of glass on east window to reduce glare

- alteration to panelling on east wall.

mber 1975	Rev. D. Nicholls leaves the parish.
er 1975	Induction of Rev. Norman Chatfield (from St. John's, Sandown, I.O.W) by Bishop of Portsmouth

July 1979	Death of Rev. Jimmy Snook .
	Rev. M. Sheffield ordained as first Assistant Curate at St. Johns.
October 1979	Purchase of 11 Laurel Road by diocese to accomodate Rev. Michael and Mrs. Lynda Sheffield.
January 1980	"Festival of Light" performed in church by 80 members of congregation.
May 1980	Jane Richards admitted as Reader.
May 1981	Jenny Lowater admitted as Reader.
November 1982	Rev. N. Chatfield appointed as Rector of Alverstoke.
February 1983	Rev. M. Sheffield resigns as curate.
3 July 1983	Induction of Rev. R.J.S. Evens (from St. Mary's Portchester). Congregation of approx. 400, with service relayed to overspill in church grounds.
July 1983	Notice Board presented by W.O. and C.P.O's Mess of H.M.S. Sultan to mark arrival of new Vicar.
3 March 1984	Installation of Peter Lowater (former St. Johns Churchwarden) as Lay Canon at Portsmouth Cathedral.
April 1984	Repositioning of Memorial Screen at West End of church. East Wall of church curtained with the paintings of the various saints to be displayed in two periods of the church year.

June 1984	90th anniversary Altar frontals for both main and side altars presented. Anniversary marked by special service and picnic lunch.
	Ordination of Rev. Michael Lloyd, followed by his appointment as curate
November 1984	Church Library established and operating under committee.
Christmas 1984	Christmas Festival held in Lockswood Centre with cast of over 100 from St. John's congregation. Festivals repeated in 1985 and 1986.
Summer 1985	Tape recordings of services produced for the benefit of the house-bound.
	"Focus" scheme introduced, whereby giving to nominated charities promoted in designated periods of the year.
August 1985	Experts advise removal of evergreen oak tree in church grounds due to damage being caused to foundations.
September 1985	Locks Heath Day Centre Group constituted.
	Small task group appointed to specify requirements for design of new Church Hall.
April 1986	Loop for the deaf installed enabling the hard of hearing to plug in and partake of service in church.
September 1986	A very complimentary report is received following the Archdeacon's visitation - "This is a lively and imaginative parish that wishes to carry the church forward into the 21st century".
	Jenny Lowater admitted as deaconess in Portsmou Cathedral to serve at St. Johns's.
October 1986	Dedication service held on opening of Ocean Sou radio station.
	Edie Grove retired as sacristan, after 20 years in th post.
	New Service pattern accepted and resulted in a n regular 6.30 Evening Parish Communion.
May 1987	Altar Rail (front section) installed.
June 1987	Rev. Michael Lloyd left the parish.
September 1987	Jane Richards ordained as Deacon at Portsmouth Cathedral.
November 1987	Application for faculty to remove stone font and install wrought iron stand to support mounted copper bowl font.
January 1988	Rev. Canon George Cutcher (retired) joins parish help on an occasional basis.
March 1988	Anne Boggust offered herself for selection as Distinctive Deacon
Easter 1988	Musical "Godspell" performed in church in aid c Church Urban Fund.
April 1988	Rev. Jenny Lowater left to officiate as a deacon Portsmouth Cathedral, to join with her husband Peter who was a Lay Canon at the Cathedral.

The "Team" (c. 1986) with the Bishop of Portsmouth
...eft, Jane Richards, Jenny Lowater, the Bishop, Michael Lloyd and Bob Evens

June 1988	Rev. Stuart Holt ordained and took up post as curate. Call by local churches for youth facilities in Locks Heath and a working party set up to explore ways in which meeting centre could be provided.
September 1988	Building Liasion Committee set up to enable Church Council to fulfil its decision to commission a scheme for extension of church and its facilities (including the Hall)
February 1989	Introduction of two new services. A monthly Family Service (1st Sunday) and Evening Praise (2nd Sunday) with an 11 a.m. Communion Service (1st Sunday). Contact Groups started, to meet in each other's houses on a weekly basis.
March 1989	Introduction of radio microphones and changes to amplifier and mixing units.
September 1989	Planning application lodged for erection of Church Hall/New vicarage, sale and development of old vicarage and provision of sufficient car-parking facilities.
November 1989	Garden of Remembrance no longer able to accomodate individual stones- a special walled area with flower bed in which ashes would be interred. Name of deceased person to be recorded in specially purchased Book of Remembrance and kept on permanent display in church.

January 1990	Large tree from vicarage garden fell and crushed a passing car. Passenger was released by emergency services unhurt. Tree crushed fencing and uprooted gas pipes. Rev. Stuart Holt left parish to join R.A.F. as chaplain.
March 1990	Pastoral Order for change of parish boundaries transferring part of parish to Sarisbury, Warsash and Titchfield. Introduction of Laying on of Hands for Healing at occasional evening service. Reported that for the first time the Apportionment had not been met.
June 1990	First edition of "Grass Roots", new-style church magazine. Rev. Jonathan Watson joins parish to begin training.
July 1990	"Proms at St. John's" performed.
September 1990	Anne Boggust ordained in Portsmouth Cathedral and started her ministry at Hook-With-Warsash
October 1990	Rev. Jane Richards appointed Asst. Chaplain at Queen Alexandra Hospital Portsmouth
November 1990	Locks Heath Money Advice Centre launched by members of local churches.
December 1990	Performance of the "Messiah" in church.
March 1991	Gift Day held in support of Church Extension Building Programme.
May 1991	Building Programme Phase One commences with erection of Church Hall - completed November 1991. Rev. George Cutcher died suddenly.
July 1991	Rev. Jonathan Watson ordained Priest at Portsmouth Cathedral.
October 1991	Rev. John Maybury licensed as Senior Curate.
January 1992	The Vicar, Rev. Bob Evens, and his family move in new Vicarage.
February 1992	Opening of new Church Hall by Mayor of Fareham with Dedication by Bishop of Portsmouth, signifying completion of Phase One of two - phased development programme. In 18 months the congregation had given or loaned nearly £200,0... "Friendly Faces" scheme set up in Church Hall to provide a friendly point of contact with a confidential drop-in listening service to people in parish. Toddlers Club and Bereavement Group set up.
February 1992	Rev. Bob Evens takes sabbatical until September France on retreat on his own for six weeks follow by working in Norfolk, Virginia, U.S.A.
March 1992	Di Townsend offered herself and was later select for ordination.
April 1992	A play "The Vigil" held in church, produced by Morgan.

vember 1992	Rev. Chris Lewis, a Minister of the Methodist Church, was invited to help at St. Johns. Rev. Bob Evens appointed as Rural Dean, Fareham.
e 1993	Bob Thomas and Sylvia Martin admitted as Readers.
1993	"Proms at St. Johns" performed.
ember 1993	"The Gift" play performed in Church, produced by Jim Wood.
uary 1994	Rev. Jonathan Watson left the parish to become Vicar in Erith, Kent.
1994	Dr. Henry Rattle joins as lay minister.
1994	Rev. Jane Richards ordained as priest in Portsmouth Cathedral. Rev. Anne Boggust rejoins parish as ordained deacon.
ember 1994	Links Scheme set up with individuals or couples providing pastoral care to small groups of the congregation.
h 1995	Centenary Reunion Lunch and Service.
1995	Parish pilgrimage to the Holy Land.
995	David Weir ordained Deacon in Portsmouth Cathedral and joins St. John's as Assistant Curate.
995	Contract signed for the construction of the new Church Centre.

St. John the Baptist, Locks Heath
1895 - 1995

ACKNOWLEDGEMENTS

I am grateful for the help, encouragement, information and material provided by Alan Babington, Anne Boggust, Trevor Cox, Evelyn Davies, Rev. Bob Evens, Norah Greenwood, Ray Greenwood, Jeff Hunter, Alma Keen, Grace Ottaway, Portsmouth City Records Office, Laurie Starks, Agnes Reading, Joan Renton, Dick Richards, Rev. Jane Richards, Marion Robinson and Lily Warmington.

My thanks to the Locks Heath Women's Institute for allowing me access to their Scrapbook being a record of the village's history up to the time of the Festival of Britain in 1951 and to Pam Jefferies for enabling me to use some pictures from that scrapbook.

I am particularly indebted to Lewis Read of Shepperton in Middlesex for the material which he provided in respect of his great-uncle Louis Lynn, much of which was the product of local research by Ray Greenwood.

My thanks to Phil Broadway for his valuable design and technical assistance.

BIBLIOGRAPHY

A Short History of Warsash by F.W.L (Spotlight 1986)

The History of Locks Heath by Trevor Cox (J. Wayles & Part.1974)

The Portsmouth Region by Stapleton & Thomas (Alan Sutton Pub.1989)

Hampshire County Magazine - June 1990 (Article "Louis Lynn and Locks Heath" by Ray Greenwood)

Peter Jeffs is married to Cherie, with two daughters Lisa and Amanda, and has lived in nearby Titchfield for many years. He is employed by an international insurance company and is a member of the St. John's congregation.

Peter is an avid football and cricket supporter and is also involved in freelance sports journalism. Two of his football books have been successfully published nationally.